Napoleon's Legacy
Wisdom for Modern Success

By John Clark

Who This Is For

For anyone ready to turn chaos into opportunity—whether you're building from scratch, reimagining your career, or scaling an existing venture. Napoleon clawed from Corsican obscurity to reshape Europe through vision, action, and calculated risk. Alex Harper transformed a passion for sustainability into a thriving business, from a $200 desk to a $2.5M enterprise. Their stories are dramatized for impact—not textbook retellings—but the principles behind them are authentic and universal.

This is for entrepreneurs and corporate innovators, side-hustlers and established owners, creatives and professionals who recognize that success isn't about aggression alone, but strategic clarity and persistent execution. The battlefield might be a boardroom, online platform, workshop, or startup—the strategic DNA remains the same.

From empires to enterprises, these lessons bridge centuries. They apply whether you're launching a digital product or building a physical business, leading a team or working solo. This isn't about ruthlessness—it's about results with purpose, about finding the edge that turns vision into reality.

For the curious, the determined, the builders who've tasted setbacks and still push forward: your path awaits—claim it your way.

Introduction: From Corsica to Your Corner—Napoleon's Playbook

Paris, October 5, 1795. Cannons cut through the smoky streets as royalist insurgents threaten to undo the Revolution. A young artillery captain with a thick Corsican accent stands before his officers, points to an "impossible" battery position at L'Éguillette, and simply says, "Here." Three hundred yards and a muddy slog later, his precisely placed guns bring the fortress to its knees—and a legend is born.

Fast-forward to Miami, 2025. Under a single garage bulb, Alex Harper chisels reclaimed oak into a charging-port desk while watching bulldozers erase his childhood woods. He sees more than splintered trees; he sees suburban professionals craving durable, sustainable workspaces—an overlooked gap he's determined to fill. His first wobbly desk isn't perfect, but it sells for $200. That messy, marginalized victory seeds a business that will break $2.5 million in revenue by marrying practical imagination with relentless execution.

Their paths share the same DNA despite centuries between them: spot the opportunity others dismiss, move with decisive speed, build systems that scale beyond personal limits.

You're next—whether you're launching a digital startup, revitalizing a career, or scaling an existing business.

This isn't about silver spoons or privileged head starts. Gates had Harvard—you've got grit and something more valuable: a proven framework. Napoleon's edge cuts through today's noise—raw, modern, chaos-to-empire principles that work in boardrooms and bootstrapped ventures alike. Vision, speed, resilience—rules that built France's throne and Alex's enterprise are yours to deploy.

What makes Napoleon's playbook different is its brutal utility. His rise wasn't blessed by gods or bankrolled by privilege—it was engineered through strategic clarity and relentless execution. Just like Alex proves two centuries later, scrolling through Reddit to identify furniture pain points while building pieces that scale from garage workshop to regional chain.

You don't need to storm the Bastille or conquer Italy. But you do need to spot gaps others miss. Hit before your rivals blink. Get up after you fall. Build systems that survive when you're not in the room. These aren't theories—they're battle-tested moves that generate real results in today's chaotic markets.

Each chapter delivers a specific principle—from vision that identifies opportunities to systems that sustain growth. Through Alex's climb from a $200 wobbly desk to a $2.5M enterprise with Napoleon's edge, you'll get a concrete battle plan for your own conquest.

This is for the builder who's tasted failure—the side-hustler going full-time, the corporate innovator seeking breakthrough, the small business owner ready to scale. Their rules—vision, speed, resilience—can turn your side hustle into a legacy or your business idea into market dominance.

You'll see Alex fail when he ignores Napoleon's lessons on overreach. You'll watch him recover by channeling the emperor's resilience. By the final page, you'll have a strategic framework tailored for your own conquest—whether that's a market niche, a revenue target, or an industry disruption.

Start with one move: spot your gap and strike.

Napoleon changed history. Alex built his empire. You're in—let's sharpen your edge.

Chapter 1: The Power of Vision - Spot the Damn Gap

"Impossible is a word to be found only in the dictionary of fools."

—Napoleon Bonaparte, Letter to General Clarke, 1816

THE BLOOD OF TOULON

Toulon, southern France, December 1793. Winter rain soaks through threadbare uniforms. Mud sucks at boots. The army of the French Republic—a ragtag mess of farmers playing soldier—shivers outside fortress walls.

The French Revolution's in chaos—royalists defect, inviting British ships to seize Toulon's harbor, a key Republican port. Napoleon's with the Republic, fighting to reclaim it from traitors and foreign invaders. If they lose, the Revolution's lifeline snaps.

Inside, royalist traitors drink wine with British naval officers. French ships bob in the harbor—stolen, now pointing cannons back at their own countrymen. If Toulon stays in enemy hands, the Revolution drowns in its own blood.

Command is a circus. Generals argue strategy while soldiers starve. Napoleon Bonaparte—twenty-four years old, barely five feet tall, his Corsican accent thick enough to draw ridicule—stands in the rain, watching.

Where they see mud, he sees a map.

Where they see impossible walls, he sees weakness.

"The harbor," he mutters, pointing to a distant fort. "L'Eguillette. Take that, we control everything."

Generals laugh. The young artillery captain keeps talking, words tumbling out fast and sharp. Measurements. Trajectories. A plan. They stop laughing.

Within days, Napoleon drags cannons through mud in the dark, repositioning each one with obsessive precision. He quizzed a local fisherman for harbor inlets, ignored the generals' maps—small intel, massive edge. He measures distances by foot, marking the ground while bullets whiz past his head. Three hundred yards shifted from the original position—the difference between failure and victory.

"Here," he orders, settling a cannon in the exact spot he's calculated. "Not there. Here."

The difference seems trivial to others. It isn't to him.

Dawn breaks. His guns roar to life. Cannonballs slam into L'Eguillette's walls with surgical precision. Stone cracks. The fort that was "impossible" to take starts crumbling.

But the royalists fight back. A counterattack surges toward the French lines. Napoleon doesn't retreat.

"Grapeshot," he commands.

Grapeshot—hundreds of musket balls packed in canvas, a brutal shotgun blast from hell—tears into bodies, shredding flesh and bone. Napoleon gives the order. Cannons belch fire.

Bodies shred. Blood sprays across cobblestones. Screams fill the air. The attack breaks.

But it's not just enemy soldiers caught in the blast. Civilians too— women, old men, children. Their bodies mix with the uniformed dead. Napoleon watches, unmoved.

He didn't create the chaos. He just saw a way through it others missed.

The fortress falls. The British fleet retreats rather than face Bonaparte's precisely positioned guns. Toulon returns to Republican hands.

Napoleon's boots squelch through blood-soaked mud as he inspects the aftermath. Victory stinks of gunpowder and gore. It isn't clean. It isn't pretty.

But it's his.

The young officer's reputation rockets overnight. "The Hero of Toulon," they call him now. The same generals who mocked his accent now listen when he speaks. Two years later, he commands the Army of Italy. In eight years, he's Emperor of France.

All because he saw a gap no one else spotted—and had the steel to take it.

THE VISION PRINCIPLE

Vision isn't what they teach in business school.

That's the edge you need—now watch Alex wield it.

It's not a mission statement framed on a wall. Not a five-year plan bound in leather. Not some mystical power granted to "visionaries" born special.

Vision is seeing the crack in chaos that others miss, then having the guts to ram yourself through it—blood and grime included.

Napoleon didn't theorize at Toulon. He didn't form a committee or hire consultants. He saw a tactical opportunity in a specific fort that nobody else valued. Then he shifted his cannons 300 yards—a small, precise change with massive impact.

That's the essence of vision: specific opportunities, concrete actions, messy execution.

Most people want clean wins. They wait for perfect conditions, risk-free entries, guaranteed success. While they wait, the true visionaries—the Napoleons of the world—are getting bloody seizing the gap.

Vision isn't magic. It's practical opportunity recognition plus unflinching action.

Napoleon didn't flinch at the blood pooling around L'Eguillette. Your vision shouldn't flinch at the mess either.

THE GARAGE GAMBLE

Miami's suburbs, 2025—hot, humid, and gritty. Alex Harper stares at the ceiling of his cubicle, counting fluorescent lights to stay awake. Eight years in corporate supply chain management has earned him a decent salary, health insurance, and a soul-crushing emptiness that follows him home every night.

Through his window, bulldozers tear into the last patch of forest in his suburb. The same woods where he built forts as a kid—now becoming another cookie-cutter development. Another McMansion monstrosity with three-car garages and marble islands nobody cooks on.

Monarch Development's banner flaps in the breeze. The same company that bought off the city council when residents protested. Alex's jaw clenches watching their CEO smile for photos with the mayor. The man destroyed something irreplaceable—and made millions doing it. The rage burns in Alex's gut like rocket fuel, driving every move he makes.

That night, in his own garage, Alex's pencil scratches furiously across paper. Not blueprints for forts this time. Desks. Tables. Bookshelves. Reclaimed wood with built-in tech—charging ports, hidden compartments for cables, solar-powered accent lights.

His neighbor Ron leans against the garage door, beer in hand. "Fancy furniture? In this economy? Good luck with that, buddy."

Alex doesn't look up. "Not fancy. Functional. Sustainable."

"People want cheap crap from big box stores. That's where the money is."

"Maybe." Alex keeps sketching. "But there's a gap."

The gap he sees: suburban professionals working from home, sick of particle board that breaks in a year, wanting something sustainable without the designer price tag. Something local. Something with a story.

He's lived with the cheap stuff—drawers that jam, handles that snap off when you pull them, shelves that sag under the weight of a few books. His wife hates how the sharp edges of a budget dresser snag her nails every morning. In the cubicle farm, nobody notices. At home, everyone does.

Alex's wife Emily walks in as Ron leaves. She studies the sketches, frowning.

"You're seriously quitting your job for this? We have a mortgage. Responsibilities."

"I've got five years of savings. I'm not asking you to risk anything."

"This is suicide. We'll lose the house." She sighs. "But at least you're not sitting around complaining anymore."

Alex's stomach twists—$200 won't cover the mortgage, but he grinds on, jaw tight.

Two weeks later, Alex's boss asks why his productivity's dropped. Instead of excuses, Alex hands in his resignation.

That afternoon, he drives to a demolition site where workers are gutting an 1890s warehouse. He talks the foreman into selling him a pickup load of old-growth oak flooring heading for the dumpster. Two hundred bucks for wood that's survived three times longer than he's been alive.

His garage becomes a workshop. The first desk takes four attempts. Joints don't align. The surface isn't level. Wood splits where it shouldn't.

But the fifth try works. Sort of. One corner's still a little wobbly, but it stands. Dark oak with clean lines. USB ports embedded in the side. A small compartment for cables. It's not perfect—far from it—but it exists.

Alex posts pictures on neighborhood social media. Waits.

Three days later, Karen from four blocks over messages him. She's starting a home business and needs a desk. Her husband bought her one from a big box store that collapsed during a Zoom call. She'll pay $200 if Alex can deliver by the weekend.

The desk wobbles when Karen leans on it. "That corner's a bit off," she notices.

Alex's stomach drops. "I can take it back, refund your—"

"I didn't say I don't want it." She runs her hand over the wood. "My grandfather had floors like this in his house. And the cable management is brilliant. When can you make a matching bookshelf?"

Two hundred dollars. Not even minimum wage for the hours he put in. But it's his first sale. Proof the gap exists.

Within a month, he sells three more pieces. Each better than the last. Each paying a little more. The wobble disappears. His cuts get cleaner. His designs more refined.

Emily stops calling him nuts. Starts helping with the books instead.

The developer clearing the forest orders a conference table for his sales center. Doesn't recognize Alex as the kid who once built forts in the trees his company bulldozed. Pays $2,000 without blinking.

Alex takes the check with a smile that doesn't reach his eyes. Uses the money to buy more salvaged wood. Hires a part-time carpenter who's sick of building identical kitchen cabinets for tract homes.

Vision isn't pretty. But it pays.

SPOTTING YOUR GAP

How do you spot that overlooked opportunity—your "gap"—and turn it into a breakthrough? Follow these principles:

Catalog persistent pain points – Listen for recurring frustrations in forums, reviews, or everyday conversations.

Map your unique assets – List your skills, resources, or connections that others underestimate.

Intersect problem & strength – Find where your assets directly solve those pain points.

Validate with a micro-experiment – Build the smallest possible prototype or pilot to test demand.

Embrace the messy win – Launch imperfectly, learn from real feedback, then refine.

Scale vision into routine – Turn your early insights into repeatable processes for idea-generation.

The strongest visions don't come from grand ideas alone—they emerge from clear, specific openings that match what you uniquely bring to the table.

THE VISION CONNECTION

Napoleon and Alex—separated by centuries but bound by the same principle. Both spotted gaps others missed or dismissed. Both took action while others theorized. Both embraced the mess that came with execution.

Napoleon's artillery shift at Toulon wasn't revolutionary—it was a specific tactical tweak others overlooked. The genius wasn't the idea; it was seeing the opportunity and seizing it while accepting the bloodshed.

Alex's eco-furniture wasn't a groundbreaking concept. Reclaimed wood has been around forever. USB ports aren't new. But he saw a specific local gap—suburban professionals wanting sustainable, tech-friendly, locally-made pieces—and filled it despite the wobbles.

Their visions weren't grandiose master plans. They were practical opportunities specifically matched to their skills and resources, executed with acceptance of the inevitable mess.

Napoleon didn't have the manpower for a conventional siege, so he found another way. Alex couldn't compete with mass-produced furniture, so he carved a niche where that disadvantage became a strength.

Both approaches reflect a common pattern:

See the specific gap others miss
Match it to your available resources
Act decisively despite the mess
Adjust through execution

Vision isn't a gift from the gods. It's a muscle you build through practice—seeing opportunities where others see obstacles, taking action while others wait for clarity.

Napoleon didn't hesitate when civilians got caught in his grapeshot. Alex didn't wait for the perfect design before selling his first desk. They saw their shots and took them, imperfections included.

That's the edge you need—the courage to spot your gap and fire into it, even when the results get bloody.

THE TAKEAWAY

See the gap, seize it—messy wins count more than perfect plans.

Napoleon shifted cannons 300 yards and changed history. Alex built a wobbly desk that launched a $2.5M enterprise. Your opportunity doesn't need to be flawless—it needs to be specific, aligned with your capabilities, and executed before others recognize it.

The perfect gap already has competition. The messy gap others dismiss is where empires begin.

While others debate ideal approaches, you move. While they wait for risk-free entry, you build. While they fear imperfection, you embrace it as the price of first-mover advantage.

Vision isn't seeing what doesn't exist; it's spotting what others overlook — and having the courage to claim it first.

Your shot won't be clean. Take it anyway.

Chapter 2: Mastering Strategy - Outsmart, Don't Outspend

"In war, three-quarters turns on personal character and one-quarter on the terrain."
—Napoleon Bonaparte, Maxims, 1831

THE FOG OF AUSTERLITZ

Austerlitz, December 2, 1805. Freezing fog blankets the battlefield. Napoleon Bonaparte stands on a small rise, watching darkness fade to gray. Below him, 73,000 French soldiers wait in the shadows. Across the valley, 85,000 Russians and Austrians prepare to crush him.

The Emperor smiles.

He's outnumbered. Outgunned. His supply lines are stretched thin. By conventional logic, he should retreat.

Instead, he ordered his men to build campfires on the heights, then abandon them. Made his army look smaller, weaker than it was. Feigned retreat for days, practically begging the enemy to advance. Throughout the night, those fake campfires burned, luring the enemy into position like moths to flame.

The enemy took the bait without hesitation.

"It's working," Marshal Davout whispers, breath clouding in the dawn air. "They're taking the Pratzen Heights. Just as you predicted."

Napoleon nods once. He saw this battlefield weeks ago—not in person, but in his mind. Every hill, every valley, every move and countermove mapped out while others slept. The Russians and Austrians think they're seizing an advantage. They're actually marching into a trap.

He turns to Davout, the most relentless of his marshals. A man who once marched his corps 70 miles in 36 hours to make a battle.

"When the sun burns away the fog, attack their flank. Not before."

Davout doesn't question the timing. The Grande Armée doesn't question orders. They execute. Every soldier has drilled these maneuvers hundreds of times, marching blindfolded across rough terrain until the formations became instinct. Some divisions can change from line to square and back in under a minute—even in darkness, even under fire.

Napoleon's generals know the plan. His soldiers know their roles. Now, they wait.

The enemy advances, dividing their forces to encircle what they believe is a retreating French army. Their center thins as they stretch for the kill.

"They're overextending," Davout says, tension in his voice. The moment approaches.

The fog begins to lift. Weak winter sunlight filters through the mist. A glowing white disk rises over the battlefield—some would later call it "the Sun of Austerlitz."

Napoleon draws his sword.

"Now."

The Grande Armée surges forward with mechanical precision. Infantry columns morph into attack lines, cavalry squadrons wheel and charge. While the Russians and Austrians focus on the French right wing, Napoleon hammers their exposed center.

The Pratzen Heights—the key to the battlefield that the enemy thought secure—becomes their death trap. French infantry smash through the weakened center. Cavalry exploit the gap, cutting the enemy army in two.

Panic spreads through Russian and Austrian ranks. Their carefully planned attack dissolves into chaos. Some flee across frozen lakes, where French artillery fire shatters the ice. Men and horses plunge into freezing water, screaming as they drown.

Blood soaks the snow. Bodies pile on the heights. By day's end, 15,000 Russians and Austrians lie dead or wounded. Napoleon loses fewer than 2,000 men.

The battle they'll call his masterpiece is over in hours.

Later, as the Emperor rides across the corpse-strewn field, an aide asks how he predicted the enemy's moves so precisely.

"Strategy isn't magic," Napoleon replies. "It's preparation meeting opportunity. They had more men, more guns. We had more discipline, better positioning."

He pauses, looking back at the Pratzen Heights, now red with blood.

"They tried to outspend me. I outsmarted them."

THE STRATEGY PRINCIPLE

Strategy isn't what they teach in MBA programs.

It's not colorful charts or bloated PowerPoints. Not market forecasts built on guesswork. Not throwing money at problems until they go away.

Strategy is outthinking your opponents when you can't outspend them—using precision and preparation to overcome brute force.

Napoleon didn't win at Austerlitz by having the biggest army. He won by drilling his men until complex maneuvers became obsessive muscle memory. By using terrain as a weapon. By making the enemy fight on his terms, not theirs.

That's the essence of strategy: turning disadvantages into advantages through positioning, preparation, and execution.

Most small players try to compete with giants on the giants' terms—more advertising, more inventory, more hype. They get crushed because they're playing the wrong game. While they bleed cash trying to match resources, the true strategists—the Napoleons of the market—are changing the battlefield entirely.

Strategy isn't expensive. It's observant. Patient. Precise.

Napoleon didn't blink at the blood freezing on Austerlitz's snow. Your strategy shouldn't flinch at the cost of victory either.

THE CRAFT FAIR GAMBIT

At Miami Beach Craft Fest, Alex Harper turns $1,500 into $3,000 in a single weekend—Napoleon's Austerlitz logic at work in the modern marketplace.

Sweaty crowds weave between booths under palm shade. Alex's $1,500 investment—his entire profit from last month—sits heavy in his wallet. Time to outsmart, not outspend.

Across the aisle, Stellar Office Supplies has the prime corner spot. Their flashy banner cost more than Alex's entire setup. Their particle board desks—the same crap that Monarch Development floods into big-box stores across Miami—gleam under professional lighting. The same company that bulldozed Alex's childhood forest now peddles furniture that crumbles under real use. An LCD screen loops polished promo videos. Two salespeople in matching polos hawk 20% discounts.

Alex has a folding table, three of his reclaimed wood pieces, and a hand-painted sign.

"You're fucked," Javier mutters beside him. The carpenter's shirt is already sweat-soaked, and it's not even noon. "They've got the spot, the setup, the staff."

"They've got overhead," Alex replies. "We've got a strategy."

For weeks, he's been preparing his battlefield advantage. Like Napoleon drilling his troops until maneuvers became instinct, Alex refined his approach through obsessive practice:

Online, he scoured Reddit threads about work-from-home furniture complaints, categorizing pain points and solutions. He joined Miami design groups on Facebook, noting which aesthetics drove engagement. He researched peak foot traffic times at previous fairs, mapping the optimal moments to engage serious buyers versus browsers.

In person, he drilled his pitch in the mirror, voice growing hoarse as he refined each line. Emily timed him, critiqued him, made him start over when he fumbled. He positioned his pieces to catch the afternoon light that makes the grain pop, testing angles until the wood's natural beauty became a silent salesperson.

The Stellar guys blast the same generic pitch to everyone who passes. Alex watches, counts. Their conversion rate is abysmal—lots of lookers, few buyers.

A couple approaches his booth—mid-30s, well-dressed, the woman scrolling through home office designs on her phone.

Alex doesn't launch into his pitch immediately. He asks questions first.

"Working from home or hybrid?"

The man looks up, surprised. "Both of us remote now. Why?"

"Because it changes how you use your space. Corporate offices are built for show. Home offices need to be built for life."

He guides them to his centerpiece—a reclaimed oak desk with built-in USB ports, hidden cable management, and a plant shelf positioned to hit the camera's sightline during video calls.

"This wood comes from a 1920s warehouse downtown. The developers were going to trash it." He doesn't mention it was Monarch Development—the same company flooding Miami with cheap furniture made from clear-cut forests. Their shadow fuels his pitch without needing their name.

The woman runs her hand over the smooth surface. "No sharp edges to catch on clothes."

"Or break nails," Alex adds. "My wife's dresser handles kept snagging hers."

He demonstrates the cable management system—no more tangled cords, no more hunting for chargers. Shows how the plant shelf not only looks good on camera but helps filter the air.

His voice never wavers. His movements are precise. Every objection they raise, he's ready for—not with desperate rebuttals, but with benefits he's drilled a hundred times.

"Our apartment doesn't have great light," the woman says.

Alex nods. "That's why I added these solar-charged accent lights. They collect enough energy by the window to give you six hours of ambient lighting away from natural light sources."

The man frowns. "It's more expensive than the ones across the aisle."

"It'll outlive them by decades," Alex replies. "When they're sending their third particle board desk to the landfill, you'll still be using this one. And unlike them, I offer free delivery and setup in Miami-Dade County."

He doesn't compete on price because he can't. He competes on value, sustainability, and service—battlefield advantages the big guys can't match.

Twenty minutes later, they're swiping their card for $1,200—nearly half his previous fair total in one sale.

By Sunday evening, Alex has made $3,000 from just ten sales. The Stellar booth, despite their $10,000 setup and prime location, sells fewer than half as many pieces—and at lower margins.

"How the hell did you outsell us?" one of their reps asks, genuinely confused.

Alex could explain his strategy—the targeted pitch, the sustainability angle, the focus on specific pain points most big-box stores ignore. But why give away the advantage?

"Just lucky, I guess," he says instead.

In the truck driving home, Javier shakes his head. "Man, you worked those people like a damn magician. Never seen someone flip a sale like that."

Alex grins. "Strategy beats spending every time."

THE STRATEGY CONNECTION

Napoleon and Alex—separated by centuries but linked by the same principle. Both faced bigger, better-funded opponents. Both used precision and preparation to create advantages their resources couldn't match.

Napoleon's victory at Austerlitz wasn't about having the most men or guns—it was about positioning, timing, and turning his soldiers' movements into obsessive muscle memory. The Grande Armée could execute complex maneuvers in fog because they'd drilled until these actions became instinct. While the Russians and Austrians relied on brute force, Napoleon created a trap they never saw coming.

Alex's craft fair win wasn't about having the biggest booth or the most inventory—it was about targeting specific customer pain points and honing his pitch through relentless practice. He trained until his presentation became second nature, allowing him to focus on reading customers instead of remembering talking points. While Stellar relied on flashy displays and discounts, Alex created value his competition couldn't match.

Their approaches reflect a common pattern:

Identify the terrain where bigger opponents are vulnerable
Prepare obsessively until execution becomes automatic
Let the enemy fight on your terms, not theirs
Use precision to overcome greater resources

Strategy isn't about resources—it's about resourcefulness. Napoleon couldn't match the combined armies' numbers, so he changed the battlefield dynamics. Alex couldn't match the big-box stores' budgets, so he highlighted sustainable values they couldn't authentically claim.

Napoleon didn't hesitate to use freezing lakes as a weapon, turning the enemy's retreat route into a death trap. Alex didn't hesitate to exploit big-box vulnerabilities—poor quality, environmental indifference, generic service—to carve his niche. They both recognized that trying to beat stronger opponents at their own game was suicide.

That's the edge you need—the discipline to find your natural advantages and exploit them ruthlessly, even when the path looks harder than frontal assault.

THE STRATEGY PLAYBOOK

How do you outthink better-funded rivals when you can't outspend them? Follow these principles:

Survey your terrain – Analyze market dynamics: customer behaviors, competitor blind spots, and emerging trends.

Identify asymmetric advantages – Pinpoint where your agility, niche expertise, or partnerships let you punch above your weight.

Drill core processes – Practice your critical moves until they become instinctive under pressure.

Design traps, not battles – Lure competitors into overreach or resource-draining tactics.

Leverage minimal resources – Use smart sequencing—small bets, big learning—to conserve capital.

Iterate based on real results – Treat every launch as data: refine positioning, adjust timing, then strike again.

Effective strategy isn't about having the biggest arsenal—it's about using the tools you have more cleverly than anyone else.

THE TAKEAWAY

Outthink, don't outspend. Master your battlefield, not your budget.

Napoleon spotted weakness at the Pratzen Heights; Alex identified what mass-produced competitors couldn't deliver. Both won by focusing resources where they created maximum impact.

Your advantage isn't money—it's focus, preparation, and strategic positioning. The terrain you choose determines your fate more than the resources you command.

While giants throw cash at every problem, you drill your approach until it's second nature. While they rely on brute force, you exploit specific vulnerabilities they're too bloated to address.

The best strategy isn't matching their strength—it's changing the rules of engagement entirely. Make them fight where size becomes a liability rather than an asset.

Blood soaked the fields at Austerlitz. Alex's hands blistered at the fair. Your path won't be painless either.

Outsmart them anyway. Or align with strategic partners who complement your edge—combining strengths to create a force greater than either could muster alone.

Chapter 3: The Speed of Conquest - Hit Before They Blink

"Take time to deliberate, but when the time for action has arrived, stop thinking and go in."
—Napoleon Bonaparte, Letter to his brother Joseph, 1806

THE BLITZ OF ULM

Ulm, Germany, October 1805. Rain hammers down for the fifth straight day. Boots sink ankle-deep in mud. Napoleon's Grande Armée—73,000 strong—pushes forward like a living battering ram.

Eighty miles in six days. Through mountains. Through storms. Through darkness.

Men drop from exhaustion. Boots shred to ribbons. Feet bleed into socks that haven't been dry in a week. Some soldiers march on raw flesh, leaving crimson footprints that wash away in the relentless rain. They advance anyway.

"The enemy expects us to approach from the Black Forest," Napoleon tells his marshals, hunched over maps in a rain-soaked tent. "So we circle north and hit their flank."

The Austrian Army, 70,000 soldiers under General Mack, waits in defensive positions, facing the wrong direction. They expect a traditional advance. A predictable siege. Time to maneuver.

Napoleon gives them none of it.

He orders night marches, boots cracking on frozen paths, to outpace scouts. Soldiers stumble through darkness, guided by drum beats they've followed a thousand times before. To their right, Marshal

Davout—the Iron Marshal—drives his corps beyond human limits, covering 70 miles in 36 hours. Men collapse. Some die. The column doesn't stop.

"When do we rest?" an aide asks.

"When we win," Napoleon replies.

While Austrian commanders debate their next move, French cavalry appears where no enemy should be—behind them, cutting off their retreat. Infantry materializes from morning fog, cannons already in position.

General Mack stares in disbelief at reports flooding his headquarters. It's impossible. No army could move this fast.

But Napoleon's army isn't just any army. It's a machine built for speed—troops trained to march faster, deploy faster, kill faster than any force in Europe.

By October 20, Mack is surrounded. The trap snaps shut before he realizes it exists. Twenty-seven thousand Austrian soldiers surrender without firing a shot. The remainder flee eastward, but they're too late. The campaign Napoleon's generals thought would take months ends in just two weeks.

Later, riding past columns of Austrian prisoners, Napoleon speaks to his blood-footed infantry.

"I said I would lead you to victory. Here it is."

A soldier with bleeding feet and hollow eyes looks up.

"Next time, Emperor, could we go slower?"

Napoleon's laugh cuts through the rain. "Speed leaves no time for the enemy to react. They were defeated before they knew they were fighting."

In his campaign journal that night, he writes words that will echo through centuries:

"Take time to deliberate, but when the time for action has arrived, stop thinking and go in."

THE SPEED PRINCIPLE

In the market as on the battlefield, the swift devour the careful.

Speed isn't about reckless rushing or thoughtless action. It's about hitting before competitors know you're coming—accepting the bloody costs of momentum over the higher costs of hesitation.

Napoleon didn't win at Ulm by having the perfect plan. He won by executing faster than his enemy could comprehend. His troops bled, suffered, even died on the march—but they reached positions the Austrians thought impossible to hold.

That's the essence of speed: accepting imperfection to seize opportunity before it vanishes.

Most small players cling to preparation, waiting until every detail is perfect before launching. They get bypassed because they're playing the wrong timeline. While they polish, the true conquerors—the Napoleons of the market—are already three moves ahead, adapting on the fly.

Speed isn't reckless. It's decisive. Committed. Unstoppable.

Napoleon didn't flinch at the bloody footprints trailing his march to Ulm. Your momentum shouldn't stumble over the inevitable mess of rapid execution either.

THE MARKET SPRINT

Four days. That's all Alex Harper gave himself to design, build, and bring three plant-friendly bookshelves to Miami's Spring Green Market. While competitors spent months perfecting prototypes, he was already setting up his booth under the March sun, sweat dripping as he positioned his imperfect but market-ready creations.

"This is insane," Javier mutters, wiping sweat from his forehead. "We built these in four days."

Three reclaimed wood bookshelves lean against Alex's booth walls. The edges aren't perfectly flush. Some of the joinery shows gaps. The finish is uneven in spots—sanded smooth but lacking the high-gloss coat of mass-produced pieces.

But each one has something unique: a dedicated plant niche with a hidden drainage system—a small tray that catches runoff, keeping roots alive and furniture dry.

"It's not about perfection," Alex replies, positioning the display piece. "It's about getting here before the season peaks."

Two weeks earlier, browsing a garden center, he'd overheard frustrated customers complaining about water damage to furniture from indoor plants. That night, a quick check of Google Trends confirmed what he'd suspected: searches for "plant water damage furniture" and "how to protect wood from plants" were spiking. A problem hiding a niche—exactly the kind of gap Alex lives to fill.

Four days of frantic design and construction followed. Emily thought he was crazy. Javier cursed the pace. Alex made brutal cuts—sacrificing the hand-carved details he'd originally sketched, abandoning a more complicated drainage system that would have taken an extra day to perfect. Some battles you lose to win the war.

The Spring Green Market—Miami's biggest eco-focused event—wouldn't wait for perfection.

"Stellar will be here next month with their catalog," Alex says, straightening a sign. "Monarch's cheap shit will flood Home Depot before summer. We hit now or lose the window."

The market opens. Foot traffic builds slowly. Alex watches shoppers pass by, notes which booths draw attention, tweaks his display angle three times in the first hour.

A woman with a collection of small potted plants slows at his booth.

"These are beautiful," she says, running a hand along the grain. "But I love plants, and furniture and water don't mix."

Alex grins. "Check this out."

He demonstrates the drainage tray, showing how it sits concealed within the shelf design but slides out for emptying. Pours a small cup of water through a test plant, catches the runoff cleanly.

"No water damage, no root rot. Everything stays healthy."

The woman's eyes widen. "How much?"

Before noon, he's sold the first shelf for $600.

By three o'clock, a line forms. Alex fields questions, demonstrates features, closes sales back to back. He adjusts his pitch on the fly, emphasizing different benefits based on customer reactions—the water tray for plant lovers, the reclaimed wood story for eco-shoppers, the sturdy construction for families.

A buyer points out a loose screw on the second shelf's plant tray.

"It wobbles a bit," the man says, frowning.

Alex doesn't hesitate. Grabs a screwdriver from his toolkit, tightens it on the spot.

"Fixed," he says with a confident grin. "Lifetime guarantee—anything comes loose, I'm a call away."

The man nods, impressed, and completes the purchase.

Emily arrives mid-afternoon with more business cards—they've run out twice already. Her eyes widen at the crowd.

"Holy shit," she whispers. "How many have you sold?"

"All but the display," Alex says, handing back change to a customer. "And that one's spoken for if I can deliver today."

By closing time, Alex has made $5,000 in a single day. Every shelf is sold. Sixteen orders are paid for future delivery.

Across the market, a Stellar Office Supplies rep scowls from an empty booth. Their polished catalog shows plant-friendly furniture— coming next season. Perfect products that don't exist beat imperfect products that do exactly never.

"How'd you know this would hit so big?" Emily asks as they load the truck.

Alex shrugs. "I didn't. But I knew waiting to find out was a bigger risk than going in fast with something imperfect."

Javier secures the display shelf in the truck bed. "Next time, can we take more than four fucking days? My hands are wrecked."

Alex laughs. "Speed leaves scars. But hesitation leaves opportunity on the table. The market rewards those who move, not those who wait for perfect."

THE SPEED CONNECTION

Napoleon and Alex—separated by centuries but united by the same principle. Both recognized that speed creates opportunities brute force can't match. Both accepted imperfection as the price of forward motion that leaves competitors scrambling to catch up.

Napoleon's victory at Ulm wasn't about superior numbers or weaponry—it was about velocity and surprise. The Grande Armée moved so fast that conventional wisdom said it was impossible. Soldiers' boots disintegrated, their feet bled, some didn't survive the march—but they reached positions before the enemy believed they could, creating an advantage no defensive strategy could counter.

Alex's market success wasn't about having the most polished product—it was about identifying a need and filling it before competitors mobilized. His shelves weren't perfect, screws needed tightening, edges weren't flawlessly finished—but they solved a genuine problem and reached customers while Stellar was still planning its catalog release.

There are limits to speed—structural integrity can't be compromised, core functionality must work. Napoleon ensured his artillery could still fire after forced marches. Alex tested his drainage system repeatedly before selling. Know what corners you can't cut, then slash everything else that slows you down.

Their approaches reflect a common pattern:

Identify an opening with a limited window
Commit fully to rapid execution
Accept the costs of speed as less than the costs of delay
Adapt and fix on the fly, never breaking pace

Speed isn't thoughtless rushing—it's calculated urgency. Napoleon spent months preparing for campaigns that executed in weeks. Alex spotted the plant-furniture gap through careful observation before his four-day building rush. Both distinguished between deliberation (where time builds advantage) and action (where time kills opportunity).

Napoleon didn't hesitate when his soldiers left bloody footprints across Germany. Alex didn't hold back when faced with imperfect shelves and the season's biggest market. They both recognized that the perfect moment never arrives—it's manufactured through decisive action that creates its own timing.

That's the edge you need—the discipline to prepare thoroughly, then the courage to "stop thinking and go in" when opportunity appears, accepting whatever mess comes with the momentum.

THE SPEED FRAMEWORK

How do you move faster than everyone else—without sacrificing your core quality? Follow these principles:

Separate planning & launch – Give yourself a strict deadline to stop planning and start shipping.

Prioritize ruthlessly – Focus on features that directly unlock customer value; defer the rest.

Build rapid feedback loops – Release in small batches, gather user reactions immediately.

Fix on the fly – Triage critical issues live, then circle back for deeper improvements.

Empower decision on the front lines – Delegate authority for minor tweaks so nothing stalls.

Learn & adapt continuously – Use each iteration to sharpen both product and process.

True speed isn't reckless haste—it's decisive action balanced with just-enough quality to learn and win before others even get started.

THE TAKEAWAY

Strike fast, fix fast, win fast. The swift own markets before the careful even enter them.

Napoleon blitzed through Germany while Austrians debated their approach. Alex dominated the Spring Market while Stellar polished their catalog. Both seized their moment with decisive action that created facts on the ground competitors couldn't undo.

Your advantage isn't perfection—it's velocity. The market you enter today is different from the one that exists tomorrow. Opportunities don't wait for refined execution or comfortable timelines.

While others polish endlessly, you move. While they wait for ideal conditions, you create them. While they fear the rough edges, you embrace them as the price of being first.

Deliberate carefully, then execute ruthlessly. When it's time to move, hesitation becomes your most expensive mistake. Your first version will have flaws—fix them in real-time while competitors are still drafting plans.

Speed isn't the enemy of quality—delay is. Napoleon's bloody-footed soldiers outmaneuvered perfectly supplied Austrians. Alex's quickly-built shelves outsold Stellar's coming-soon catalog.

Perfect readiness is an illusion. When the window is closing, strike now—polish later.

Chapter 4: Leadership Under Pressure - Hold the Line, Heart and All

"The leader is the arbiter of the people's fate."
—Napoleon Bonaparte, Letter to the Directory, 1796

THE CRUCIBLE OF ITALY

"The Directory sent a boy to fix this mess?"

The general's sneer cuts through the air as Napoleon Bonaparte, twenty-six and newly appointed commander, dismounts his horse. Before him stretches not an army but a collection of human wreckage—the once-proud Army of Italy reduced to 30,000 starving, unpaid men in rags.

April 1796. The French Republic's Italian campaign teeters on collapse. Soldiers desert daily. Those who remain huddle in miserable camps, uniforms rotting, stomachs empty. Supply wagons abandoned. Morale shattered. Officers drinking away what little remains in the treasury.

The young Corsican doesn't waste time with the sneering general. Instead, he walks directly to the common soldiers—gaunt, filthy, desperate men who've heard too many empty promises.

"Soldiers," Napoleon says, voice carrying despite its softness. "You are hungry. You are naked. The government owes you much but can give you nothing."

Murmurs ripple through the ranks. This new general at least speaks truth.

"I will lead you into the most fertile plains in the world," Napoleon continues. "Rich provinces, great towns will fall into your power. There you will find honor, glory, and wealth."

The men stare, disbelieving. Italy—defended by Austrian armies, Piedmontese fortresses—seems an impossible conquest.

But something in the young general's eyes makes them listen. Something in his voice makes them believe. Not just his words, but the absolute certainty behind them.

Within days, Napoleon implements three tactical leadership moves that transform the army. First, he institutes a direct communication chain, bypassing corrupt officers to speak with unit commanders daily. Second, he creates a meritocracy, promoting soldiers who show initiative regardless of background. Third, he establishes clear mission objectives with tangible rewards for each town captured.

He institutes night marches—50-mile treks through mountain passes the enemy believes impassable. Men drop from exhaustion, but those who remain grow stronger, tougher.

"The general marches with us," a soldier tells his comrades after Napoleon refuses a dry tent, choosing instead to sleep in the same mud as his men. "Not like the others."

At Montenotte, they smash a Piedmontese force. At Mondovi, they seize their first major city. With each victory, Napoleon does exactly as promised: the spoils go first to the men, their pockets filling with coins, their bellies with food.

Murat, his cavalry commander, rides at the front of every charge, saber flashing, bleeding but relentless. When hit by grapeshot at Dego, he binds his wounds and leads the next assault. The men see it all—the officers bleed first, eat last.

Napoleon demands discipline while sharing the hardship. Executes looters but rewards bravery. The Army of Italy transforms from a starving mob into a fighting machine fueled by devotion to the general who turned their fate.

"I found them mud-covered beggars," Napoleon writes to Paris. "I return them warriors."

By the campaign's end, they've conquered northern Italy, smashed four Austrian armies, captured 150,000 prisoners, and seized priceless art for France. What began as a desperate gamble ends as Napoleon's defining triumph.

Years later, when asked how he inspired such steadfastness, Napoleon replies simply:

"Men will die for glory, honor, or a leader's fire—not for five francs a day."

THE LEADERSHIP PRINCIPLE

Leadership isn't granted by title—it's forged in fire.

When chaos erupts and resources vanish, fancy management theories collapse. What remains is the primal truth of leadership: people follow conviction backed by results, not position backed by authority.

In Italy, loyalty came from Napoleon's unshakable purpose, not his rank. He transformed starving deserters into conquerors through presence in hardship, clarity in mission, and dedication to their success. His leadership technique—what military strategists now call "shared hardship leadership"—created bonds that no official power could match.

The essence of leadership is making others believe when evidence suggests otherwise, then delivering victories that validate their faith. It's standing at the front when retreat seems logical. It's sharing the worst conditions while demanding the highest standards.

Most entrepreneurs confuse management with leadership. They create structures, assign responsibilities, track performance—all necessary, but insufficient when pressure mounts. While they design systems, true leaders—the Napoleons of business—forge tribal connections that withstand chaos.

Leadership costs nothing in capital but everything in commitment. It requires no fancy degree but demands complete conviction. It isn't about being perfect—it's about being present when stakes are highest.

Napoleon's nights in Italian mud forged an army; Alex's nights under a leaking warehouse roof prove the same truth—leadership is earned through shared struggle, not proclaimed from comfort.

THE WAREHOUSE CRISIS

"We're finished."

Emily's voice breaks as she hands Alex the letter. Monarch Development has bought their workshop building. Thirty days to vacate. No renewal option.

Six months of growth, fifteen active orders, nowhere to build them. Their small operation—Alex, Emily, Javier, and two part-time assistants—faces extinction just as they're gaining momentum.

"They're doing this deliberately," Alex says, recognizing the developer's name. The same company that bulldozed his childhood forest, now targeting his business. "They've seen our growth. We're a threat to their cheap furniture line."

Javier slams his chisel down. "Three years of my life. Back to building cookie-cutter cabinets." The two assistants exchange glances, already planning their exits.

Alex studies their faces—defeat settling in before they've even fought. The same expression he'd seen on customers stuck with disposable furniture. The same look of resignation that meant accepting less than what was possible.

"Meet me at this address tomorrow morning," he tells them, scribbling on the back of the eviction notice. "Six AM."

"Why?" Emily asks.

"Just be there."

Dawn breaks as their cars pull into the cracked parking lot of an abandoned warehouse on Miami's industrial edge. Graffiti covers faded brick walls. Broken windows gape like missing teeth. The property has been derelict for years.

"What are we doing here?" Javier asks, not bothering to hide his irritation.

Alex unlocks the rusted side door. "Just follow me."

Inside, dust motes dance in beams of light streaming through holes in the roof. Pigeons scatter from rafters. The concrete floor is stained with decades of industrial spills.

But the space is vast—10,000 square feet of potential where others see only decay.

"This is our new workshop," Alex announces.

Emily laughs, bitter and sharp. "You can't be serious. This place is condemned."

"Not anymore," Alex says, producing a folder. "I bought it yesterday. The inspection cleared this morning."

Silence falls as they process his words.

"With what money?" Javier finally asks.

"Every dollar I have. And a loan against my house."

"You're insane," Emily says. "We have thirty days to complete fifteen orders. We need a functioning space now, not a restoration project."

Alex walks to the center of the cavernous room. "I slept here last night. Mapped every square foot. The electrical's solid. Plumbing needs work but the main lines are good. This section," he indicates the cleanest area, "can be operational in three days."

"Impossible," Javier mutters.

"Napoleon crossed the Alps in six days," Alex replies. "We can make this warehouse operational in three."

He outlines his plan—three focused days to create a minimally viable workspace in one corner. Complete existing orders while gradually expanding into the rest of the building. Use the crisis to scale instead of retreat.

"This is your solution?" Emily asks, disbelief in her voice. "Risk everything on a wreck when we could just rent a temporary space?"

"Temporary spaces make temporary businesses," Alex says. "This will be ours. No landlord. No eviction. While Monarch thinks they're killing us, we're building an arsenal."

He walks to each team member in turn, looking them directly in the eyes. "I know it looks impossible. But I'll be here every hour of every day until it works. I need you, but I understand if you walk."

The team stands motionless, weighing risk against possibility.

Javier breaks first, walking the perimeter, measuring with his eyes. "The ceiling height is better than our old place," he admits grudgingly. "Natural light too, once we clean those skylights."

One of the assistants, Miguel, points to the northeast corner. "Loading dock's intact. That saves us on material handling."

Small observations. Tiny surrenders to hope.

"Three days," Emily says finally. "If we can't build here in three days, we find another solution."

Alex nods. "Fair."

They work without stopping. Alex sleeps on-site, running electrical lines while others sleep. Javier brings his own tools, then his brother's, then his cousin's. Emily negotiates with suppliers for same-day deliveries, calling in every favor they've earned.

On day three, Monarch's property manager calls to verify their move-out date.

"We've already relocated," Emily tells him calmly. "You can keep the security deposit."

By nightfall, a 1,000-square-foot corner of the warehouse hums with activity. Two workbenches. Basic tools. A makeshift office. Not pretty, not perfect—but functional. Their first on-site build, a conference table for a law firm, takes shape under Javier's careful hands.

When that first piece ships on time, something shifts. The team doesn't see a ruined warehouse anymore. They see the foundation of something bigger than what they lost.

Two weeks later, they've expanded to 3,000 square feet of operational space. A month after that, they've completed not just the original fifteen orders but twelve more. The crisis that should have destroyed them instead forced an evolution.

On the day they would have been evicted from their original workshop, Alex gathers the team—now eight people strong.

"I want to show you something," he says, leading them to a wall where he's hung their first dollar, earned from that wobbly desk sale months ago.

Beside it hangs a new document—the warehouse deed, marked PAID IN FULL.

"How?" Emily asks. "The loan was for three years."

"Remember those law firm partners who bought the conference table? They ordered executive desks for their entire office. Thirty-two pieces. Paid in advance."

Javier whistles low. "Because?"

"Because I told them our story. How Monarch tried to shut us down. How we refused to die. How every piece we build is a middle finger to disposable culture." Alex's eyes flash. "They bought our mission, not just our furniture."

The warehouse still needs work. Rain still leaks through sections of the roof. But it's theirs. Unconquerable.

Emily studies the deed, then looks at Alex. "When you brought us here that first day, did you know we'd actually pull this off?"

Alex considers this. "I knew we had to. The 'how' just had to catch up with the 'must.'"

That night, long after the others have gone, Javier finds Alex patching a leak in the roof.

"You know," Javier says, "I thought you were full of shit that first day."

Alex laughs. "You weren't wrong."

"Maybe," Javier concedes. "But I would've missed this." He gestures to the transformed space below. "Next time you lead us into insanity, count me in earlier."

It wasn't pretty. But it worked.

THE LEADERSHIP CONNECTION

Napoleon and Alex—separated by centuries but united by the same principle. Both faced existential crises, skepticism, and the pressure to deliver. Both transformed desperate situations into victories through vision, shared struggle, and tangible results.

Napoleon's triumph in Italy wasn't just military genius—it was leadership alchemy. He took starving, demoralized troops and forged them into a conquering force not through superior resources, but through being present in their hardship, clear in his vision, and relentless in delivering victories that benefited them all. When Murat charged with saber drawn despite his wounds, it reinforced Napoleon's culture of shared sacrifice.

Alex's warehouse transformation wasn't just entrepreneurial survival—it was leadership in action. He rallied his team not through authority or promises, but by confronting reality head-on, committing personally to the struggle, and creating an environment where crisis became opportunity. When he slept in the derelict building while others went home, it demonstrated his absolute commitment to the mission.

Napoleon slept in the mud alongside his men; Alex spent nights repairing the warehouse roof while his team rested. Both understood that leadership presence—physically sharing hardship with those you lead—creates bonds that authority can't match.

Their approaches reflect a common pattern:

Articulate a clear, compelling vision that serves everyone
Share in the struggle, demonstrating skin in the game
Deliver tangible wins that reward the faith of followers
Build attachment through actions, not just words

Leadership isn't about being liked—it's about being followed. Napoleon's men didn't adore his personality; they believed in his ability to deliver victory and the spoils that came with it. Alex's team didn't always agree with his methods; they trusted his capacity to create opportunities that benefited them all.

Napoleon didn't hesitate to demand discipline alongside sacrifice. Alex didn't shy away from pushing his team past their comfort zones. Both understood that true leadership balances pressure with purpose, drive with direction.

That's the edge you need—the courage to hold others to high standards while demonstrating through your own actions that the struggle leads to meaningful reward.

THE LEADERSHIP BLUEPRINT

How do you lead under pressure so people follow you through thick and thin? Follow these principles:

Be present in hardship – Share the toughest conditions to earn genuine buy-in.

Clarify the mission – Spell out not just goals, but why they matter to each team member.

Empower merit – Reward initiative and results, regardless of rank or background.

Share the spoils – Distribute wins—credit, rewards, recognition—to those who made them happen.

Enforce standards with fairness – Hold everyone, yourself included, to the same rules.

Rally around small victories – Celebrate progress to sustain morale when stakes are high.

Real leadership isn't about issuing orders—it's about forging shared conviction through shared struggle and shared success.

THE TAKEAWAY

Lead from the front, win as a team. Conviction creates followers.

Napoleon slept in Italian mud before asking troops to march. Alex risked his savings before asking his team to commit. You earn the right to lead through action, not position.

Your leadership isn't built on authority—it's forged through demonstrated conviction and shared success. People follow those who prove the path is possible, not those who merely point the way.

When pressure mounts, presence matters more than polish. Be physically where the challenge is greatest. Take the same risks you ask of others. Show through your actions that you value mission over comfort, results over appearance.

Leadership under pressure requires both steel and heart—the resolve to hold the line when others waver, and the humanity to remember why the line matters. Your team doesn't need a perfect leader; they need one who stands with them when stakes are highest.

Vision without execution breeds cynicism. Execution without vision breeds burnout. Combine them, and genuine commitment follows—not blind allegiance, but the earned trust of people who've seen your words become their reality.

Chapter 5: Resilience in Defeat - Get Up, Swing Again

> "From triumph to downfall is but a step. I have seen a trifle decide the most important events."
> —Napoleon Bonaparte, Memoirs of St. Helena

THE FALL AND RISE

Elba, May 1814. A small Mediterranean island becomes the prison of a fallen emperor.

Napoleon Bonaparte—once master of Europe, commander of millions—paces the limited grounds of his diminished domain. His empire crumbled. His Grande Armée destroyed in Russia's snow. His marshals have abandoned him. The allies who feared him now mock him. King Louis XVIII, a member of the Bourbon royal family that ruled France before the Revolution, sits on France's throne.

It was total defeat.

For weeks, he hardly leaves his quarters. Servants find him staring at maps of campaigns he'll never fight, fingering medals from victories that no longer matter. The island governor reports to allied powers that the great Napoleon is broken at last.

Then something shifts.

A visitor finds him one morning planning harbor improvements. The next day, he's reorganizing the island's tax system. Within a month, he's built a miniature court, established mines, improved roads, and transformed his tiny kingdom.

"You seem to have accepted your fate, Emperor," the British commissioner observes.

Napoleon's eyes flash. "Fate is not finished with me, monsieur. Nor I with it."

On February 26, 1815, he makes his move. While his guards distract British ships, Napoleon boards a small brig with 1,000 loyal soldiers. The force is pitifully small—an army that once numbered 600,000 reduced to a battalion of scarcely a thousand men. But every man is committed to their leader's cause.

They land near Antibes. The path to Paris lies before them, guarded by royalist troops. At Grenoble, they encounter the 5th Regiment— guns aimed at Napoleon's small force.

Napoleon dismounts. Walks alone toward the wall of bayonets.

"Soldiers of the 5th," he calls, opening his coat. "If there is one among you who wishes to kill his Emperor, here I am."

Silence. Then a roar erupts: "Vive l'Empereur!" The royalist troops drop their weapons, rush to their former leader.

Word spreads. Regiment after regiment defects. The Bourbon king flees. Within 20 days of landing, without firing a shot, Napoleon reclaims Paris. The impossible restoration is complete.

"How did you know they wouldn't shoot?" an aide asks later.

"I didn't," Napoleon replies. "But after Elba, bullets held no fear. One either lives caged by defeat or risks everything to rise again."

The victory is temporary. Napoleon knows the allied powers will come for him. Russia, Prussia, Austria, Britain—all mobilize massive armies. At Waterloo, ten months later in 1815, his final gamble fails. He is exiled again, this time to the remote island of St Helena, a prison he will never escape.

Yet in those Hundred Days between exiles, he demonstrated the principle that defined his career: resilience isn't about avoiding defeat—it's about refusing to accept it as final.

Years later, dictating his memoirs on St. Helena, he reflects: "In defeat, I found what truly cannot be defeated—the will to rise once more."

THE RESILIENCE PRINCIPLE

Every empire faces its Russia. Every conqueror meets their Waterloo.

The myth of unbroken success is just that—a myth. The path to victory runs directly through defeat. What separates legends from footnotes isn't perfection—it's persistence.

Resilience is the art of transforming terminal points into turning points. It's not about escaping failure—it's about refusing to let failure define what comes next.

Napoleon didn't escape defeat in Russia or ultimate exile, but his return from Elba demonstrated a truth that applies beyond battlefields: the game isn't over until you accept it's over. What looks like the end can become a pivot point if you refuse to stay down.

Most go-getters feel shame in defeat. They hide their failures, flee their fields, rebuild somewhere else. They lose momentum because they're playing to preserve image over substance. While they lick wounds, the true builders—the Napoleons of resilience—are already planning their next campaign from the rubble of the last.

The strongest approach to setbacks follows a specific pattern—what psychologists now call "transformative resilience":

Acknowledge reality without self-deception
Allow yourself a defined period of grief—hours, not weeks
Conduct a ruthless assessment of remaining assets
Make decisions based on future potential, not past loss

Resilience isn't pretty. It's raw, desperate, often ugly—rebuilding with whatever's left when everything else burns away. It's not about having enough strength; it's about continuing when strength is gone.

In a world obsessed with overnight success, the competitive edge belongs to those who can endure overnight disaster.

THE BETRAYAL AND COMEBACK

"All of it? Every single piece?" Alex stares at his phone in disbelief.

"Flooding wrecked it all," Marco says, too calm to believe. "Three inches of water overnight. Look man, I'm sorry, but nothing's salvageable."

Alex grips the edge of his workbench. Marco's warehouse—where $20,000 worth of Alex's finished pieces wait for delivery—supposedly flooded overnight. Three bookshelves, two desks, four coffee tables. All the Rodriguez family's conference table. All the custom work for the neighbors. Every piece from the warehouse launch.

"When can I come see it?" Alex asks, voice tight.

A pause. "There's nothing to see. Insurance already hauled it away."

Something in Marco's tone doesn't match his words.

Two hours later, Alex pulls up to a different warehouse across town. A contact in the delivery business tipped him off: Marco never had a flood. He's been selling Alex's furniture through a side channel, cutting Alex out completely.

Through the warehouse window, Alex sees his pieces—the distinctive live-edge desks, the plant-shelf bookshelves—being loaded into a truck with Stellar Office Supply's logo. The same competitor from the craft fair.

Inside the workshop, Emily and Javier wait for news. Their faces fall when Alex walks in, shoulders slumped.

"Gone?" Emily asks.

"Worse. Stolen." Alex explains Marco's betrayal, the Stellar connection. Twenty thousand dollars of finished work—gone. Orders to refund. Customers to disappoint.

"We're fucked," Javier mutters. "That was everything we had ready."

Emily stares at their bank balance on her tablet. "We can't afford to rebuild all that inventory."

Alex slumps onto a stool. The room spins slightly. Three months of work. Their entire ready-to-deliver stock. All their momentum from the warehouse transformation—gone.

For a moment—just one—he considers walking away. Going back to a steady paycheck. Admitting the dream was just that.

Then his gaze falls on a small photo tacked to the wall: the forest of his childhood, before Monarch's bulldozers. Next to it, a newspaper clipping announcing Monarch's newest development: a chain of eco-themed cafés selling cheap, pseudo-sustainable furniture.

"Monarch Developments Launches 'GreenSpace' Café Chain," the headline reads. "Bringing sustainability to Miami hospitality."

Using green marketing to sell the same disposable crap.

Something in his vision snaps into focus.

"We pivot," he says, standing so abruptly that Javier flinches. "Right now."

"To what?" Emily asks. "We have nothing to sell."

"We have the one thing Marco can't steal—our skill." Alex grabs a pencil, starts sketching rapidly. "Javier, remember that modular shelving system we talked about? The one that assembles without tools?"

Javier nods slowly. "The interlocking joints? That was just an idea."

"No, it's our next product line. Simple components we can produce fast, that customers can configure themselves."

Emily frowns. "Who'd buy furniture they have to assemble?"

"People who can't afford custom but still want quality." Alex's pencil moves faster. "We cut one-third from our prices, deliver twice as fast, still use reclaimed materials."

Javier looks skeptical but moves to the workbench. "We'd need to standardize everything."

"Exactly. Five components, endless configurations. We replace complex with clever."

Alex faces a critical decision fork: pursue legal action against Marco or pivot to a new model. Like a tech startup choosing whether to sue over stolen code or launch a better product, he evaluates both paths in terms of time, energy, and potential return.

"What about suing Marco? Getting our inventory back?" Emily asks, voicing the obvious.

"Lawyers cost money we don't have. Courts take time we can't spare," Alex replies. "By the time we win a case, our customers will have moved on. Speed beats revenge."

For three days, they barely sleep. Alex and Javier prototype while Emily hunts new materials sources. They abandon Marco's supply chain completely, partner with a local salvage co-op instead.

"They'll take a higher cut," Emily warns.

"But they won't steal our designs," Alex counters.

Seven days after Marco's betrayal, they have a new line: Modulo—reclaimed wood furniture that ships flat, assembles without tools, costs 40% less than their custom work. The craftsmanship's still there, just redistributed into the connection system rather than bespoke designs.

"Now we need customers," Emily says. "Fast."

Alex thinks of Monarch's eco-café announcement. "If you can't beat the bastards, infiltrate them."

He calls every independent café in Miami. Pitches Modulo as sustainable furnishing that reflects their values without breaking their budgets. Most hang up. Three agree to meetings.

The first two pass. The third—Groundwork Coffee, with three locations—picks up a sample shelf, tests the assembly.

"How fast can you outfit our new location?" the owner asks. "We open in three weeks."

Alex doesn't hesitate. "We'll have it ready."

Back at the workshop, Javier explodes. "A whole café? In three weeks? Impossible."

"We streamlined production, remember? Standardized components."

"For shelves and side tables—not for seating, not for service counters."

"So we adapt. Fast."

They work around the clock. Alex refines designs during the day, helps Javier build at night. Emily handles logistics, material sourcing, delivery scheduling. They hire two part-time helpers—both craftspeople Javier knows—and teach them the system.

Two days before the deadline, they deliver and assemble: twelve tables, thirty chairs, six bar stools, a modular service counter, and wall shelving throughout. All from reclaimed wood. All assembled on-site with Groundwork's staff helping.

The café owner runs his hand along a table edge. "This is remarkable. Our customers will ask where we got it."

"We're counting on that," Alex says.

By the end of the month, they've made $30,000—more than they lost in Marco's betrayal. Two more cafés place orders. A coworking space inquires about furnishing their new location.

In the workshop, Emily updates their business plan. "Commercial clients are more profitable than residential. Faster payment, larger orders."

"And they value the story," Alex adds. "The sustainability angle matters to their brand."

Javier, sketching a modified chair design, looks up. "Imagine Marco's face when he sees our stuff in cafés all over town."

Alex grins. "He thought he'd finished us. Instead, he forced us to evolve."

What looked like destruction became the catalyst for transformation.

THE RESILIENCE CONNECTION

Napoleon and Alex—separated by centuries but united by the same principle. Both faced betrayal, loss, and the temptation to surrender. Both transformed potential endings into new beginnings through sheer refusal to accept defeat as final.

Napoleon's psychological journey on Elba parallels Alex's after Marco's betrayal. Both experienced initial shock and isolation—Napoleon staring at maps of past campaigns, Alex slumped on his workshop stool. Both allowed themselves a brief period of despair before making the decisive mental shift from victim to strategist.

Both conducted ruthless assessments of remaining assets—Napoleon his reputation and loyal followers, Alex his skills and team.

Napoleon's return from Elba wasn't just a military maneuver—it was psychological warfare against the very concept of defeat. With just 1,000 men, he reclaimed an empire because he understood that most barriers exist primarily in the mind. When royalist troops aimed guns at him near Grenoble, his willingness to risk everything rather than accept exile broke through their psychological resistance.

Alex's pivot after Marco's betrayal wasn't just a business strategy—it was a declaration that his vision couldn't be stolen along with his inventory. By redesigning both his products and his market approach in days, he demonstrated that resilience isn't about recovering what was lost, but building something new from what remains. When he approached café owners instead of replacing his residential customers, he turned necessity into opportunity.

Resilience isn't about avoiding pain—it's about refusing to let pain have the last word. Napoleon's greatest defeat in Russia became the setup for his most audacious return. Alex's inventory loss forced a product and market innovation that might never have happened otherwise.

Both men understood that defeat is often just success in disguise—if you have the courage to unwrap it.

THE RESILIENCE FRAMEWORK

How do you turn a crushing defeat into the springboard for your next triumph? Follow these principles:

Acknowledge reality quickly – Face the loss head-on without denial.

Limit your grief window – Give yourself a set, brief time to process, then refocus.

Inventory remaining assets – List skills, relationships, and resources still on your side.

Identify pivot opportunities – Look for new angles or adjacent markets you can attack.

Build a lean rebound plan – Prioritize actions that deliver the fastest, highest-leverage returns.

Execute with humility – Accept help, solicit feedback, and iterate as you rebuild.

Resilience isn't about avoiding failure—it's about refusing to let failure define what comes next.

THE TAKEAWAY

Defeat is temporary. Surrender is permanent.

Napoleon turned exile into a comeback that shook Europe. Alex transformed betrayal into innovation that expanded his market. You make defeat the catalyst, not the conclusion.

Your advantage isn't absence of failure—it's response to it. In a world where most quit after the first serious blow, resilience becomes your market advantage. The capacity to absorb punishment and keep moving isn't just admirable—it's profitable.

Know when to persist and when to pivot. Fighting to recover what's lost often costs more than building something new. The strongest resilience isn't blind persistence but strategic adaptation—identifying when the path forward requires a new direction rather than just more force.

When everything falls apart, focus not on what's lost but what remains. Skills. Knowledge. Relationships. The core that can't be taken from you becomes the foundation for what comes next.

Resilience isn't pretty. It's not inspirational quotes over sunset photos. It's the raw, desperate scramble back to your feet when everything says stay down. It's the decision to turn dead ends into detours, not destinations.

Napoleon's army crumbled in Russia's snow. His empire vanished in exile. Alex's inventory disappeared in betrayal. His business plan collapsed overnight. Neither let these moments define their story.

Your defeats will come. Your Russia awaits. Your Marco will betray.

Get up anyway.

Chapter 6: The Double-Edged Sword - Ambition's Gut Punch

"Great ambition is the passion of a great character. Those endowed with it may perform very good or very bad acts. All depends on the principles which direct them."
—Napoleon Bonaparte, Letter to Josephine, 1796

THE FROZEN ABYSS

Russia, June 1812. The largest army ever assembled in European history crosses the Niemen River. Six hundred thousand men. Twenty thousand carriages. Eighty thousand horses. A moving city of muskets, cannon, and hunger for glory.

At its head rides Napoleon Bonaparte, Emperor of France, master of a continent. With most of Europe subdued, only Russia still defies him, refusing his Continental System against British trade.

"Six weeks," he tells his generals. "We'll be in Moscow in six weeks."

His generals exchange glances. Marshal Davout—the Iron Marshal—speaks what others won't.

"Winter comes early in Russia, sire. If we haven't won by October..."

Napoleon cuts him off with a wave. "The Russians will give battle long before then. One decisive victory, and Tsar Alexander will sue for peace."

But the Russians don't give battle. They retreat, burning crops, poisoning wells, leaving scorched earth. Napoleon's supply lines stretch thinner with each mile. His massive force begins to disintegrate before firing a shot.

"We should establish winter quarters," his quartermaster advises in August, "Prepare for the cold months ahead."

"No," Napoleon snaps. "Moscow will capitulate, and we'll winter there."

By September, they reach Borodino. The Russians finally stand and fight. Victory costs Napoleon thirty thousand men, but the road to Moscow lies open.

On September 14, the Grande Armée enters Russia's ancient capital. They find it eerily empty. That night, fires erupt across the city. Within days, three-quarters of Moscow burns to ash. There will be no comfortable winter quarters. No negotiated peace.

For five weeks, Napoleon waits in the charred ruins, expecting the Tsar to capitulate. His letters go unanswered. Supplies dwindle. The first snow falls.

On October 19, reality can no longer be denied. Napoleon orders retreat.

Too late.

Winter descends with murderous cold. Temperatures plunge to thirty below zero. Men freeze in their sleep. Horses collapse by thousands. Starving soldiers resort to eating leather from their own equipment.

The once-mighty army disintegrates into a desperate mob stumbling westward. Russian Cossacks harass their flanks, cutting down stragglers. At the Berezina River, they must build bridges under enemy fire. Thousands drown trying to cross.

Napoleon abandons what remains of his army, racing ahead in a sleigh to prevent political collapse in Paris. Of the 600,000 who marched into Russia, fewer than 30,000 stagger out.

Years later, his most loyal general asks what went wrong.

"I believed my own legend," Napoleon admits. "I thought my ambition had no limits because it had never found them before."

He pauses, haunted by memories of frozen corpses lining the retreat route.

"I forgot that all swords cut both ways."

THE AMBITION PARADOX

Ambition is the rocket fuel of empire-builders—and the poison that destroys them.

The same force that drives conquest beyond ordinary limits eventually pushes beyond possible ones. The line between the two is razor-thin and visible only after it's crossed.

When controlled, ambition converts obstacles into opportunities. When unleashed, it transmutes opportunities into disasters. The higher you climb, the harder it becomes to distinguish between bold vision and fatal delusion.

Napoleon didn't fail in Russia because his ambition was too small. He failed because it escaped the constraints of strategic reality. The same drive that built his empire consumed it—the supreme confidence that had served him in victory betrayed him when it dismissed clear warnings.

The most dangerous moment for any builder isn't failure—it's unchecked success. When every gamble pays off, when every critic is silenced by results, the guardrails of caution crumble. The fall becomes inevitable not despite previous triumphs, but because of them.

Like a tech startup that raises millions on AI promises it can't deliver, unchecked ambition prioritizes vision over viable execution. The company announces features their engineers haven't built, chases markets they don't understand, and burns through capital before reality arrives to collect.

The edge that separates legends from cautionary tales isn't ambition's presence, but its governance. The ability to unleash it against opportunity while leashing it against folly. To recognize when the sword is cutting for you versus into you.

THE SHOWROOM GAMBIT

Miami Design District, December 2025. Floor-to-ceiling windows gleam under track lighting. Inside, Alex Harper arranges furniture on polished concrete floors. His new showroom—1,800 square feet in the city's most exclusive design neighborhood—opens tomorrow.

"Fifty thousand dollars a month," Emily mutters, reviewing their lease. "Plus build-out costs."

"We can afford it now," Alex replies. The success with Groundwork Coffee had snowballed. Five more café clients in two months. The Modulo line featured in a local design blog. Revenue hitting $120,000 in November.

"Barely," Emily counters. "This eats almost all our profit."

"It's how we scale to the next level." Alex adjusts a reclaimed oak conference table, his new premium line dubbed 'Legacy.' No more modest café furnishings—these pieces rival designer brands at designer prices.

The café pivot had worked brilliantly, but Alex's ambition stretched beyond coffee shops. His Instagram feed filled with high-end design influencers showcasing minimalist luxury pieces in multimillion-dollar homes. Each post getting thousands more likes than the honest café work his team produced. The algorithm pushed him toward luxury, and his ambition followed.

He wanted to compete with high-end sustainable furniture brands. To put his designs in luxury homes and corporate headquarters. To show Monarch Development what true eco-luxury meant.

From the workshop corner, Javier eyes a chair's joinery. "These need another week of work."

"We don't have another week," Alex responds. "The opening party's tomorrow."

Javier crosses his arms. "These aren't café tables, Alex. At these prices, people expect perfection."

"They'll get it. And they'll pay for it." Alex checks his phone—the digital marketing campaign he's launched costs $50,000 for the month, targeting luxury clients and interior designers.

Emily and Javier exchange glances. They've seen this intensity before—Alex's ambition in overdrive, consequences be damned.

"We should stick with what's working," Emily suggests. "The café market isn't saturated yet. We're still below the revenue ceiling we agreed on before scaling."

During their warehouse days, they'd established clear guardrails: no expansion until they maintained $150,000 monthly revenue for six consecutive months with 30% profit margins. They were still three months short of that target.

"The real money is upmarket," Alex insists. "We've proven the concept. Now we scale."

The next evening, the showroom gleams. Catering servers circulate with champagne. A photographer captures product shots. The space looks magnificent.

But it's nearly empty of guests.

"Where is everyone?" Alex mutters, checking his watch. The showroom opening should have drawn dozens of designers and potential clients.

Emily checks the RSVP list. "Only three confirmed. And none have shown."

Outside, Miami traffic crawls past indifferently. The carefully targeted marketing campaign—aimed at high-end clients who've never heard of Alex's brand—has generated clicks but no conversions.

What Alex couldn't see: established luxury brands had quietly pressured designers to skip his opening. Several had received calls reminding them of existing relationships and exclusive discounts. In the high-end market, newcomers weren't just ignored—they were actively blocked.

By nine o'clock, they're alone with untouched canapés and warm champagne.

"Design district was a mistake," Javier says, stating the obvious. "Our people aren't here."

Alex stares out the showroom windows at a sleek furniture store across the street. Its owner—tanned, designer-suited—smirks while locking up, having watched their empty event all evening.

The next morning, reality crystallizes when their first month's credit card processing statement arrives. Online traffic up 300%. Actual sales down 70%. The marketing campaign targeting luxury clients has driven away their core customers while failing to attract new ones.

Alex sits alone in the empty showroom, staring at numbers that don't lie. Fifty thousand in rent. Fifty thousand in marketing. Build-out costs nearing eighty thousand. Three months of operation would wipe out everything they've built.

His phone buzzes. A notification from the Miami Business Journal: "Monarch Development Opens First 'GreenSpace' Café to Acclaim."

The article shows Jorge Mendez—Monarch's CEO—cutting a ribbon at a minimalist café furnished with mass-produced "sustainable-inspired" furniture. The same company that bulldozed Alex's childhood forest now capitalizes on eco-friendly marketing while producing disposable garbage.

Alex had been so focused on competing with high-end brands that he'd abandoned the market niche where they were actually winning. Tried to fight on terrain that favored established players with deeper pockets. Overreached just like—

"Napoleon in Russia," he mutters.

That afternoon, he calls an emergency meeting at the workshop. Emily brings the financials. Javier brings the production backlog report.

"We fucked up," Alex says without preamble. "I fucked up."

Neither argues the point.

"The showroom was my mistake. The luxury pivot was my mistake. The marketing spend was my mistake."

Emily nods. "So what now? We're locked into the lease."

"We're not." Alex points to a clause Emily herself had insisted on—a 30-day exit option if sales targets weren't met. "It costs us the deposit, but we can walk away."

"And do what?" Javier asks.

"Go back to what worked." Alex pulls out his sketchbook, flips to a fresh page. "But better."

Over the next three days, they dismantle the showroom. Return to their original workshop space. Alex calls every café client, recommits to their needs, offers upgrades on existing installations.

Then he approaches Groundwork's owner with a proposition: convert part of the showroom into a "maker space" within their newest location. Customers can watch furniture being built, even participate in workshops.

"Experiential retail," Alex explains. "People don't just want sustainable furniture—they want connection to how it's made."

The owner loves it. Two other café clients request similar setups.

Within three weeks, they've pivoted back to their core market—but with a stronger value proposition. Revenue rebounds. The marketing budget redirects to targeted local campaigns and in-store experiences.

By February, they've recouped December's losses. By March, they hit $180,000 in monthly revenue—50% more than their pre-showroom numbers.

One afternoon, Emily finds Alex staring at the design district lease cancellation paperwork.

"Still hurts?" she asks.

"Yes," he admits. "But necessary pain."

"The new direction is working better anyway," she points out. "Sometimes ambition needs guardrails."

Alex nods. "Some boundaries aren't meant to be crossed."

"And you can build something amazing without a fancy showroom."

He rolls up the paperwork, tosses it in the recycling bin. "Aim high—"

"But not blind," she finishes.

THE AMBITION DIAGNOSTIC

How do you know when ambition is propelling you forward versus pushing you off a cliff? Ask yourself:

Am I ignoring data that contradicts my vision? When Napoleon dismissed reports of Russian winter, his ambition had become delusion.

Have I abandoned metrics that previously guided my decisions? Alex ignored the six-month revenue target he had set himself.

Am I chasing status over strategy? The prestige of the Design District became more important than the strategic fit.

Are trusted advisors unified in their concerns? When both Emily and Javier express the same reservations, that's a warning signal.

Am I accelerating because of opportunity or ego? Napoleon invaded Russia for continental dominance, not strategic necessity.

When three or more questions yield uncomfortable answers, your ambition might be cutting the wrong way.

THE AMBITION CONNECTION

The emperor and the entrepreneur followed parallel paths. Napoleon stormed across Europe until ambition led him into Russian winter. Alex built a thriving business until the same force pushed him into luxury waters too deep to navigate. In both cases, the qualities that forged success—boldness, confidence, relentless drive—ultimately threatened everything they'd built.

Napoleon's conquest of Europe stemmed from brilliant ambition channeled through strategic discipline. Each campaign built on the last, each victory expanded his possibilities—until Russia. There, ambition broke free from reality's constraints. The same confidence that had served him in a hundred battles betrayed him when it dismissed clear warnings about Russian winter, extended supply lines, and scorched-earth tactics.

Alex's business growth came from ambitious vision focused on specific market opportunities. Each pivot built momentum, each success expanded his reach—until the showroom gambit. There, ambition overcame strategic sense. The same drive that had found profitable niches betrayed him when it pushed into territory that favored established competitors.

Ambition isn't the villain in either story—unchecked ambition is. The difference between Napoleon before Russia and Napoleon in Russia wasn't the scale of his goals but the governance of his drive. The difference between Alex's café pivot and his showroom gambit wasn't the boldness of his vision but the strategic soundness behind it.

Both men discovered that ambition functions like fire—essential for progress, fatal when uncontained. Napoleon's empire burned in Russian snow because he couldn't recognize when his ambition had outpaced reality. Alex's expansion nearly collapsed when he confused scaling up with moving upmarket.

That's the edge you need—not taming ambition, but harnessing it. Knowing when it's propelling you forward versus when it's pushing you off a cliff.

THE TAKEAWAY

Aim high, not blind. Your vision creates possibilities—your boundaries ensure survival.

Napoleon marched into Russia without limits. Alex leaped upmarket without foundations. You push with purpose, not just passion.

Your advantage isn't the scale of your ambition—it's the discipline that directs it. The market rewards bold moves within strategic boundaries. The same drive that builds empires destroys them when it escapes the constraints of reality.

Recognize the threshold where ambition crosses from fuel to poison. Listen to the advisors you trust—especially when they're telling you what you don't want to hear. Track the metrics that matter, not just the ones that feed your vision.

Set specific guardrails before expansion: revenue targets sustained over defined periods, profit margins that must be maintained, customer acquisition costs that can't be exceeded. When you violate your own standards, you've crossed from ambition to recklessness.

Ambition without guardrails isn't courage—it's recklessness. The line between visionary and delusional isn't drawn by the size of the goal but by the soundness of the path.

Napoleon's bones froze in Russian snow. Alex's showroom stood empty on opening night. Your ambition will find its limits too.

The question isn't whether you'll hit the wall—it's whether you'll recognize it before you shatter against it.

Chapter 7: Propaganda and Perception - Spin It, Own It

"Four hostile newspapers are more to be feared than a thousand bayonets."
—Napoleon Bonaparte, Letter to Talleyrand, 1805

THE BULLETINS OF GLORY

Marengo, Italy, June 14, 1800. Powder smoke blurs the afternoon light; spilled blood turns bare earth slick. By mid-afternoon, the situation appears hopeless.

Napoleon Bonaparte, recently installed as First Consul of France, watches his army crumble before Austrian forces. His generals urge retreat. The battle—and perhaps his rule—seems lost.

Then, salvation: General Desaix arrives with fresh divisions. A desperate counterattack turns the tide. By evening, the Austrians flee, leaving the field to the French.

Victory, but barely. Costly. Chaotic. Almost accidental.

The next morning, Napoleon sits at a field desk, penning what will become known as the "Bulletin of the Army of Italy." His quill scratches across paper, not recording history, but creating it.

In his account, there is no near-defeat. No desperate gamble. The casualties—actually close to equal on both sides—become grossly imbalanced in his favor. The chaotic fight transforms into a brilliant strategic plan executed flawlessly.

"Let the bulletin be copied and dispatched to Paris immediately," he orders.

A courier raises a question: "The casualty figures, General—"

"Are as written," Napoleon interrupts, gaze unwavering.

Within days, his version of Marengo floods Paris. Newspapers reprint the bulletin verbatim. The public celebrates in the streets. Artists begin rendering the "masterful victory" in oils. Poets compose verses celebrating the triumph.

When conflicting reports trickle in weeks later, few notice. The narrative has set like concrete.

Back in his headquarters, Napoleon establishes a system. Each military campaign will have its own bulletins, issued directly from his headquarters, controlling every detail of how battles are perceived. They will go first to Paris, then to newspapers across Europe.

"Facts matter less than the story people believe," he tells his secretary. "History is a set of lies agreed upon by those who weren't there."

Years later, he commissions paintings depicting him calmly crossing the Alps on a rearing stallion—though in reality, he crossed on a mule, bundled against mountain cold. He orders monuments showing victories while minimizing defeats. His image appears on everything from coins to wallpaper.

After each campaign, he ensures public displays of captured enemy standards and cannons in Paris churches. Tangible proof of glory that ordinary citizens can see and touch.

"Let them say what they want about me," he remarks while reviewing a critical pamphlet. "They cannot stop what they believe they've seen."

When a minister suggests suppressing all critical voices, Napoleon shakes his head.

"Censorship reeks of fear; drown criticism beneath a tide of praise instead."

By the time he crowns himself Emperor in 1804, the mythology has eclipsed the man. Perception now outweighs reality itself. A military leader from minor Corsican nobility has transformed into the heir of Charlemagne—not through bayonets alone, but through the relentless shaping of public narrative.

"In war, perception is the final battlefield," he tells his marshals. "The enemy may know they fought well, but if the world believes they were crushed, they may as well have been."

THE PERCEPTION PRINCIPLE

Reality exists, but image rules.

What people believe shapes markets, drives decisions, and determines value more powerfully than objective facts. The gap between what is and what seems to be represents the most crucial territory for any conqueror to control.

Perception isn't just about lies or manipulation—it's about strategic emphasis. Highlighting strengths. Contextualizing weaknesses. Shaping the narrative frame through which others interpret your actions.

Napoleon didn't win at Marengo through bulletins, but his artful recasting of a near-disaster into a masterful victory multiplied the battle's impact beyond its military significance. His control over how events were perceived translated battlefield success into political capital, public support, and strategic advantage.

That's the essence of perception management: not creating a fantasy, but curating which parts of reality dominate the narrative.

Most small players focus exclusively on improving their product or service, then wonder why superior offerings lose to inferior ones with better stories. They fail to recognize that reputation isn't secondary to reality—it is a reality in itself, one that determines whether other realities get seen.

The edge isn't fabrication. It's selective elevation of truth that serves your goals. It's understanding that how something is perceived often matters more than what it objectively is.

Like crafting a viral thread on X that reshapes public opinion, effective narrative control amplifies impact far beyond your actual resources. What matters isn't just what happened, but what story people believe about what happened.

Spin truth, not lies—authenticity ultimately wins. Napoleon's bulletins emphasized real victories, even as they reframed near-defeats. The most sustainable narrative strategy highlights actual strengths rather than inventing fictional ones.

THE NARRATIVE CAPTURE

Miami, April 2026. Alex Harper's workshop buzzes with activity. Six employees now, including Javier supervising production and Emily managing operations. The café business has expanded to fifteen locations. Monthly revenue holds steady at $200,000.

But something's missing.

"Monarch's GreenSpace cafés are everywhere now," Alex says, scrolling through Instagram. Their competitor's expansion has been aggressive—twelve locations in six months, all furnished with mass-produced "eco-style" pieces that merely imitate sustainability.

"We know their stuff is garbage," Javier replies. "Veneered particle board that falls apart in a year."

"But their marketing is brilliant," Emily adds. "Look at their engagement numbers."

Monarch's Instagram feed shows sleek cafés with carefully staged photos. Every caption emphasizes their "commitment to sustainability" and "eco-conscious design." Comments gush about how "green" the spaces feel.

The perception completely contradicts reality—the same company demolishing forests to build developments now positions itself as an environmental champion through furniture that will end up in landfills.

"Their story is beating our substance," Alex mutters.

That night, he can't sleep. Around 2 AM, he heads to the workshop. In the corner sits a bookshelf they're struggling to sell—a beautiful piece with slight imperfections in the finish. Alex runs his hand over the reclaimed cypress, feeling the history in its grain.

An idea forms.

The next morning, he gathers the team. "We're launching a content strategy today. Not marketing—storytelling."

He outlines a multi-channel approach. The centerpiece: a series called "Wood Has Roots" that traces each piece of furniture back to its origin.

"We start with this," he says, pointing to the imperfect bookshelf. "We document everything—where the wood came from, who built it, how it's constructed. No hiding flaws, no glossy perfection. Raw, real craft."

Emily looks skeptical. "People want perfect products in perfect settings."

"No," Alex counters. "People want authenticity. They want connection to what they buy. Monarch sells an image of sustainability. We'll show the real thing, imperfections included."

They begin that weekend. Alex brings the bookshelf to his friend's porch—overlooking the same canal where Monarch bulldozed trees. Using just a smartphone, they film the bookshelf being installed, plants being arranged on its shelves, morning light hitting its imperfect finish.

Alex narrates the story: how the cypress came from a 1930s church being demolished, how Javier spent hours hand-joining each piece, how the slight color variations show its authenticity rather than hiding it.

"This isn't furniture," his voiceover concludes. "It's resurrection."

They post the three-minute video across platforms. By Monday morning, it has 5,000 views. By Wednesday, 25,000. A local sustainable living influencer shares it, then a national one. Comments flood in, not about the product specs, but about the story.

"Where can I get one?" becomes the most common question.

"It's working," Emily says, watching the engagement metrics climb. "But we need a system to capitalize on this."

They develop one rapidly:

Each new piece gets its own origin story video
Weekly workshop tours showing production in progress
Customer spotlights featuring their pieces in use
Before/after comparisons of reclaimed materials

The strategy extends beyond social media. YouTube features become local news segments. A regional morning show invites Alex to demonstrate "furniture resurrection" live. Each appearance amplifies their story to new audiences who might never have seen their social content.

When a commenter questions whether their pieces really last, Alex doesn't defend with words. He posts a time-lapse video of Javier jumping on a Modulo table, then loading it with weights. The visual proof is more persuasive than any claim.

For their most expensive commission yet—a complete restaurant outfitting—they document the entire process from salvage to installation. The restaurant owner, initially nervous about the

$120,000 investment, becomes their biggest advocate after being featured in the content.

"You've made my business part of a bigger story," he tells Alex.

When a negative review appears—a customer complaining about color inconsistency in a tabletop—Alex doesn't hide it or argue. He creates a video explaining why reclaimed wood varies in tone, how each mark tells the material's history, and offers to replace the piece or provide a refund.

The customer keeps the table and becomes a vocal supporter.

Three months into the strategy, monthly sales hit $300,000. Their content has created a community, not just a customer base. People don't just want the products; they want to be part of the narrative— the resurrection of materials others discard.

Monarch notices. Their marketing team launches a "Craftsmanship Series" showing workers in clean workshops building furniture. But the staging feels obvious, the narrative inauthentic.

Behind the scenes, Monarch goes further. Internal emails leaked to Alex reveal their strategy: "Discredit Harper's authenticity." They begin planting negative comments questioning wood sourcing. They approach former clients offering discounts to switch suppliers and give negative testimonials.

"They're copying our approach without understanding it," Emily observes. "You can't fake authenticity."

At a design conference, Alex runs into Jorge Mendez, Monarch's CEO. The man who bulldozed his childhood forest now courts the same eco-conscious clientele.

"Your videos are quite compelling," Mendez says, sipping champagne. "But eventually people want perfection, not stories about flaws."

Alex smiles. "Maybe. But people can spot the difference between real and staged authenticity."

"Perception is reality," Mendez counters.

"Yes," Alex agrees. "But authenticity outlasts manipulation every time."

That night, Alex posts a video of reclaimed cypress being installed in a new café. In the background, visible through the window, stands a Monarch development where trees once grew. He never mentions it directly—just lets the visual tell its own story.

The comments explode with connections viewers make themselves. The contrast goes viral in Miami's design community. Three Monarch clients approach Alex within a week.

"Narrative isn't just telling stories," Alex tells his team. "It's creating frames that help people see what matters."

THE PERCEPTION FRAMEWORK

How do you shape the narrative around your work without compromising authenticity? Follow these principles:

Find your truth anchors - Identify the genuine strengths in your product, service, or story that can become foundations for your narrative

Create context, not fantasy - Frame these strengths within a story that gives them meaning beyond their functional value

Show, don't tell - Use visual evidence and demonstration rather than claims and assertions

Convert weaknesses to character - Reframe imperfections as evidence of authenticity or uniqueness

Build narrative infrastructure - Create systems that consistently deliver your story across multiple channels

Let others carry your message - The most powerful narratives spread through third-party voices, not your own

The strongest perception strategies don't fabricate reality—they highlight aspects of reality that might otherwise go unnoticed or unappreciated.

THE PERCEPTION CONNECTION

The military strategist and the furniture maker discovered the same truth: in the battle for minds, narrative power often trumps raw resources. Both understood that controlling how people interpret reality is as important as shaping reality itself.

Napoleon's bulletins about Marengo weren't pure fiction—the French did ultimately win the battle. By controlling which aspects of reality dominated the narrative, he transformed a costly, chaotic engagement into a cornerstone of his legend.

Alex's content strategy wasn't deceptive—his furniture really was built from reclaimed materials with craftsmanship Monarch couldn't match. But by creating a narrative frame that highlighted the meaning behind imperfections rather than hiding them, he transformed potential weaknesses into compelling strengths. The story about resurrection gave customers a purpose beyond the purchase itself.

Perception management isn't about denying reality but selecting which realities get prominence. Napoleon didn't hide that battles occurred, but controlled how they were interpreted. Alex didn't pretend his furniture had no imperfections, but reframed those imperfections as evidence of authenticity.

Both understood that people make decisions based not on exhaustive analysis of facts, but on the story those facts seem to tell. Napoleon's subjects didn't experience his battles directly; they experienced the narrative of those battles through bulletins, art, and monuments. Alex's customers couldn't personally verify sustainable sourcing; they experienced it through content that connected them to the materials' journey.

That's the edge you need—not just creating quality products or services, but shaping the perceptual context in which others experience them.

THE TAKEAWAY

Frame truth powerfully. Control your story.

Napoleon turned near-defeat into legend through bulletins. Alex transformed imperfections into selling points through authentic storytelling. You frame reality so its best truths define perception.

Your advantage isn't fabrication but strategic emphasis. The market responds not just to what you make, but to the story it tells. When that story resonates authentically, customers don't just buy products—they join narratives.

Control your narrative or others will define it for you. Every product, service, or idea exists in a perceptual framework. Either you deliberately craft that framework, or you surrender it to competitors, critics, or chance.

Napoleon's myth outlived his defeats. Alex's story outsold Monarch's budget. Your narrative can overcome greater resources when it captures what people want to believe.

Perception isn't everything, but everything is perceived through it.

Chapter 8: Every Man Has His Price - Buy the Win

"A man will fight harder for his interests than for his rights."
—Napoleon Bonaparte, Maxims, 1831

THE COUP OF CALCULATION

Paris, November 9, 1799 (18 Brumaire in the revolutionary calendar). France's government—the Directory—teeters on the edge of collapse. Four years of corruption and battlefield defeats have hollowed the Republic.

Napoleon Bonaparte, recently returned from Egypt, moves through the shadows of power. Today, he will seize control of France—not primarily through force, but through a precise calibration of what each key player truly wants.

"The plan proceeds tomorrow," his brother Lucien tells him. "But General Augereau still hesitates."

Napoleon nods, unsurprised. Augereau—a tough, capable general—has publicly supported the Republic. His participation would legitimize the coming coup, but his principles stand in the way.

"Arrange a private meeting," Napoleon orders. "Tonight."

When Augereau arrives at Napoleon's residence, they speak not of politics or patriotism, but of property. Napoleon casually mentions estates being redistributed, opportunities for those who recognize shifting tides. By meeting's end, a bag containing 50,000 francs changes hands—officially a "loan" between old comrades.

"France needs stability above all," Napoleon says as they part. "Those who help create it shall find their own positions most stable."

Augereau leaves committed to the cause.

But Napoleon understands that different men value different currencies. For General Bernadotte—restless and politically shrewd—Napoleon dangles command of the Army of the West, the post that will launch him toward Sweden's throne. For the intellectual Sieyès, it's the chance to implement his constitutional theories—Napoleon promises him a leading role in the new government (a promise soon broken).

For officers, he arranges promotions. For politicians, appointments. For the wealthy elite, protection of property. For common soldiers, back pay and improved conditions.

"Every lock has its key," he tells his brother Joseph. "One must simply determine which key fits which lock."

On the coup's morning, he addresses troops who will secure Paris: "The Directory has failed you—no pay, no supplies, no glory. Follow me, and France will reward your service."

When the Council of Elders resists the takeover, Napoleon marches grenadiers into their chamber. Some council members flee through windows to escape. Those who remain find their protests silenced by bayonets.

By evening the Directory lies dissolved; within three weeks (December 1799) the Constitution of Year VIII elevates Napoleon to First Consul—de facto ruler of France. Within five years, he crowns himself Emperor.

Years later, when asked how he succeeded where others failed, Napoleon explains: "The Revolution taught me that men will rarely die for abstract principles. But they will move mountains for concrete advantages. I simply matched the right advantage to the right man."

When his minister questions the morality of such methods, Napoleon replies, "I didn't create human nature. I merely recognized it."

In his personal notes, he is more direct: "Men are moved by two levers only: fear and self-interest. When one understands what moves a man, one controls him."

THE MOTIVATION MATRIX

Everyone has a price. But it's rarely just money.

The most sophisticated conquerors understand that human motivation forms a complex matrix—financial gain is merely one dimension. Power, recognition, security, revenge, belonging, legacy—each serves as currency for different personalities in different situations.

Influence doesn't come from offering what you value, but what they value. The gap between what someone publicly claims motivates them and what actually drives their decisions represents the most crucial territory for strategic advantage.

Like a digital marketer identifying the right influencers for product promotion, strategic influence requires understanding not just reach and demographics, but the unique motivational profile of each target. One influencer values exclusive access, another prioritizes creative freedom, while a third simply wants maximum compensation—each requiring a tailored approach.

Napoleon didn't win his coup through superior force—the military balance in Paris was precarious at best. He won by meticulously mapping each key player's true motivational structure, then offering precisely what would tip them toward his cause. Not just bribes, but a customized package of incentives that spoke to each individual's unique hierarchy of desires.

That's the essence of strategic influence: recognizing that everyone has their price, but the nature of that price varies dramatically from person to person and context to context.

Most small players approach influence transactions simplistically—offering the same incentives to everyone, usually based on what would motivate themselves. They fail to recognize that the key to moving others lies not in universal appeals but in personalized ones that align with each individual's particular motivational profile.

The edge isn't manipulation. It's perceptiveness—the ability to see what truly drives others and align your offers accordingly. To recognize that appeals to abstract principles usually fall before concrete advantages matched to specific desires.

THE MOTIVATION ASSESSMENT

To identify what truly moves someone, assess these three core drivers:

1. Material desires - Beyond basic compensation, what tangible benefits matter?

Financial security vs. growth potential
Immediate rewards vs. long-term stability
Ownership and equity vs. guaranteed income

2. Status and recognition - How do they define success and self-worth?

Public acclaim vs. peer respect
Formal titles vs. actual influence
External validation vs. internal standards

3. Purpose and meaning - What gives their actions significance?

Community impact vs. personal achievement
Creative expression vs. structured accomplishment
Ethical alignment vs. practical outcomes

When these three dimensions are understood, you can craft offers that speak directly to someone's true priorities rather than your assumptions.

THE LUMBER LEVERAGE

Miami, August 2026. The warehouse feels like an oven despite industrial fans pushing humid air around stacked lumber. Alex Harper examines a pallet of reclaimed wood—century-old heart pine from a demolished hotel. Perfect for the café chain contract they're bidding on.

"It's the last batch," says Vince Rodriguez, owner of Heritage Salvage. "Hotel's gone, nothing left after this."

Alex runs his hand along the aged grain. "We need twice this amount for the Sunrise Café contract. There's really no more?"

Vince shakes his head. "Already promised the rest to Westwood Design. They've been a client for three years, order every month."

Alex feels a cold knot form in his stomach. Westwood is the preferred vendor for Monarch's GreenSpace cafés—their biggest competitor. Without this wood, Alex's bid to furnish fifteen new Sunrise Café locations falls apart. A $180,000 contract hangs in the balance.

"Westwood's picking it up tomorrow," Vince adds. "Already paid half."

Back at the workshop, Alex breaks the news to Emily and Javier.

"Can we source similar wood elsewhere?" Emily asks.

Javier shakes his head. "Not in this time frame. Not with this character."

"So we offer Vince more money," Emily suggests. "Simple."

Alex frowns. "It's not that simple. Vince has worked with Westwood for years. Our relationship is newer. If we just throw cash at him..."

"Then what?" Emily presses.

Alex spends the night researching Vince Rodriguez and Heritage Salvage. Reviews their social media, business filings, community involvement. By morning, he has a picture not just of Vince's business, but of what drives him.

Heritage Salvage started as an environmental mission, not just a business. Vince left construction after seeing tonnage wasted in demolitions. His company diverts materials from landfills, but rarely gets recognition for its environmental impact.

And there's something else—Vince's son attends design school at Miami-Dade College, specializing in sustainable materials.

Alex calls an emergency team meeting. "We're not just buying wood. We're buying into Vince's vision."

He outlines a three-part approach:

Offer to feature Heritage Salvage prominently in their "Wood Has Roots" content series, showcasing Vince's environmental impact
Propose a paid internship for Vince's son at their workshop
Commit to a longer-term purchasing relationship, not just this one contract

"And yes," Alex concludes, "we'll pay a 15% premium over Westwood's price. But that's the least important part."

Emily looks skeptical. "Is this manipulation?"

"No," Alex replies. "It's alignment. Everything we're offering benefits both sides. We're not lying or exploiting—we're finding mutual interest."

That afternoon, Alex meets Vince at a Cuban café near the salvage yard. Over coffee, he presents his proposal—not as a bribe to break the Westwood deal, but as a partnership that serves Vince's deeper motivations.

"Your company deserves recognition for its environmental work," Alex says. "And your son deserves experience with craftspeople who share his values."

Vince studies him. "Westwood pays reliably. They're steady."

"They're also supplying Monarch's cafés," Alex counters. "The same company clearing forest for developments. Your wood's going to greenwash their image."

Something shifts in Vince's expression. "I didn't know that."

"Check their Instagram. Their furniture is in every Monarch GreenSpace café."

Vince is quiet for a long moment. "My son would really get to work with Javier? He's been following your content."

"Full paid internship. Real experience, not coffee runs."

"And the premium price?"

"Fifteen percent over Westwood's, with a two-year purchasing commitment."

Vince drums his fingers on the table. "I'd have to return Westwood's deposit. Make an enemy."

"We'll cover that too," Alex says. "Consider it our investment in a partnership."

Three days later, the heart pine is delivered to Alex's workshop. The cost: $15,000 premium plus covering Westwood's $7,500 deposit. The return: a $180,000 contract with Sunrise Café, a reliable wood source, and an eager intern with fresh design ideas.

In his private thoughts, Alex justifies outbidding Westwood not just as a business move, but as a moral stand against Monarch's environmental destruction. By securing this wood for genuine sustainability rather than "greenwashing," he's redirecting resources toward their proper use.

When Westwood's angry owner calls, Alex doesn't gloat or apologize.

"Business is business," he says simply. "Everyone makes their choices."

The real complexity comes two weeks later, when word gets around about how Alex secured the wood. Jorge Mendez, Monarch's CEO, mentions it pointedly at a chamber of commerce meeting.

"Interesting tactics your company employs," he says within earshot of several potential clients. "Undercutting established relationships."

For a moment, Alex feels exposed—his methods laid bare in public. Then he straightens his shoulders.

"We offered a supplier something his previous buyer couldn't— alignment with his values. That's not undercutting. That's understanding what truly matters to your partners."

Later, examining his reaction, Alex realizes something has shifted. Six months ago, he would have felt guilty about the deal with Vince—viewed it as somehow dirty or manipulative. Now he sees it differently: as strategic alignment based on genuine understanding of human motivation.

"Napoleon wouldn't have hesitated," he tells Emily when discussing the encounter with Mendez. "He would have seen it as simply recognizing reality."

"Is that who we want to be?" she asks. "Napoleon?"

Alex considers this. "We want to win. But we do it by finding real alignment, not exploitation. That's the difference."

The Sunrise Café contract leads to three more. By year-end, their commercial division has grown 40%. Vince's son designs a new shelving system that becomes their best-selling café product. The "Wood Has Roots" feature on Heritage Salvage drives sustainability-minded clients to both businesses.

Two years later, when Westwood faces bankruptcy after Monarch drops them for cheaper overseas suppliers, Vince recommends they hire Westwood's best craftspeople. The relationship that began as competition evolves into integration, strengthening both businesses.

"Everybody got what they wanted," Alex tells his team. "That's not manipulation—that's strategy with integrity."

THE INFLUENCE CONNECTION

The general and the furniture maker discovered the same truth: understanding what truly drives people creates influence that brute force can never match. Both recognized that effective persuasion comes not from imposing your will, but from aligning your offers with others' authentic motivations.

Napoleon's coup succeeded not because he had the strongest military position, but because he methodically mapped what each key player truly valued, then crafted personalized appeals. For Augereau, financial security through direct payment. For Bernadotte, position and status through command. For Sieyès, ideological fulfillment through constitutional role. By recognizing these different "currencies," he transformed potential obstacles into active supporters.

Alex's lumber deal succeeded not because he simply outbid a competitor, but because he researched what truly mattered to Vince beyond money. Environmental recognition through content features. Family advancement through his son's internship. Value alignment by revealing the Monarch connection. By understanding these deeper motivations, he transformed a transaction into a partnership.

Strategic influence isn't about manipulating others against their interests. It's about deeply understanding their true interests and creating alignments that serve both sides. Napoleon didn't force generals to support him; he showed them how their personal ambitions could be fulfilled through his rise. Alex didn't trick Vince into breaking his deal with Westwood; he offered a partnership that better served Vince's core values.

Both understood that appealing to abstract principles—patriotism for Napoleon, business loyalty for Alex—rarely succeeds against concrete advantages aligned with personal desires. The Directory's appeals to revolutionary ideals fell before Napoleon's targeted incentives. Westwood's established relationship collapsed when Alex offered Vince recognition and opportunity for his son.

That's the edge you need—not forcing others to comply through pressure, but motivating them to commit through alignment. Understanding that influence flows not from power but from perception of mutual advantage.

THE TAKEAWAY

Understand motives, align incentives. Everyone has a true price.

The path to influence lies not in pushing harder, but in identifying what truly drives decisions. When you recognize what someone genuinely values—beyond what they claim motivates them—you gain an advantage others miss.

Strategic influence requires three steps: discover what truly matters to key players, craft offers that align with those priorities, and deliver results that confirm your understanding. This approach builds lasting partnerships rather than temporary transactions.

Look beyond obvious motivations. Money matters, but rarely alone. Status, security, recognition, relationship, legacy, validation—each serves as currency in human exchanges. The most effective strategist identifies which currency holds highest value for each person in each context.

Create genuine alignment, not manipulation. Sustainable influence comes from serving others' interests while advancing your own. Napoleon's empire eventually collapsed partly because he defaulted on too many promises. Alex's partnerships strengthened because he delivered real value to all sides.

The most powerful question isn't "How do I make them do what I want?" but "What do they truly want, and how does that align with my goals?"

Napoleon secured Paris with promises tailored to each key player. Alex won a supplier with a combination of environmental recognition, opportunity for family, and fair compensation. Your path requires understanding which incentives matter most in your context.

Everyone has their price. Your edge comes from recognizing it's rarely what it first appears to be.

Chapter 9: Building an Empire - Systems That Survive

"My maxim has always been: a career open to all talents, without distinction of birth."
—Napoleon Bonaparte, Speech, 1804

THE ARCHITECTURE OF EMPIRE

Paris, 1804. France emerges from revolutionary chaos. The Terror's guillotines stand silent. The country breathes again—not in freedom, but in order.

Napoleon Bonaparte, now Emperor, sits at his desk eighteen hours a day. His generals command armies, but Napoleon commands something more fundamental: the machinery of state itself.

"Laws without systems to implement them are merely words on paper," he tells the Council of State. "Systems without competent people to run them are merely diagrams on charts."

The Emperor's greatest conquest isn't a battlefield or territory—it's the transformation of how France functions. The Napoleonic Code replaces hundreds of conflicting legal traditions with a single, coherent system of civil law. Property rights, family relationships, and commercial transactions all gain predictability.

But laws are just the beginning. Napoleon rebuilds France's infrastructure—roads, bridges, canals—standardizing design and maintenance. He reforms education with the creation of lycées that train France's future administrators based on merit, not birth. The Bank of France stabilizes currency. Prefects extend central control to distant provinces.

"A bureaucracy," one minister complains privately.

"A framework," Napoleon corrects him. "The difference between a mob and an army isn't the individuals—it's the structure that organizes them."

He institutes a tax system of unprecedented efficiency. Where tax collection once leaked revenue through corruption and inefficiency, his reforms create predictable flows to the treasury. Marshal Murat, commanding the National Guard, enforces compliance where needed.

The nobles hate it—their privileges diminished. The church resists—its authority challenged. But merchants, professionals, and ordinary citizens find stability after years of chaos.

Napoleon works through the night reviewing reports on everything from road maintenance to school enrollments. His aides marvel at his capacity to absorb detail, but miss what truly distinguishes his approach: his genius lies in designing for messy reality, not academic theory.

"Systems must work with human nature, not against it," he tells his Council. "A system that requires men to be angels will fail. A system that channels self-interest toward greater goals will endure."

He builds redundancies where corruption might emerge. Creates checks where power might concentrate. Implements feedback mechanisms where intelligence must flow. His administrators learn that results matter more than intentions—outcomes over ideology.

Most crucially, he balances centralization with delegation. Core standards come from Paris, but implementation adapts to local conditions. His prefects receive clear objectives with flexible means.

"I can conquer," he tells his brother Jerome, "but conquests crumble. Systems remain."

Years later, after Waterloo, after exile, after Napoleon's death on distant St. Helena, his enemies dismantle his empire. They restore old borders, old dynasties, old titles.

But they cannot dismantle his systems.

The Code Napoleon spreads across Europe and beyond. His administrative structures persist under new names. His educational reforms become models worldwide. When France rebuilds after his fall, it does so on frameworks he designed.

In the end, his most enduring victory wasn't won with cannons, but with systems that outlasted both his triumphs and his defeats.

THE SYSTEMS IMPERATIVE

Empires rise on vision but endure on structure.

The transition from conquering to governing represents the most critical inflection point for any builder. The same improvisation and personality-driven leadership that creates breakthrough opportunities will strangle growth without systematic approaches to sustain it.

Systems aren't sexy. They lack the drama of bold gambits or creative breakthroughs. But they possess a quality more valuable than either: sustainability independent of their creator's presence.

Napoleon didn't secure his place in history primarily through military genius, but through administrative vision that transformed how government functioned. His systems worked because they balanced theoretical elegance with practical reality—recognizing human limitations and incentives while creating structures that channeled them productively.

That's the essence of effective system-building: designing frameworks that capture your best thinking, align individual incentives with collective goals, and function reliably without constant personal intervention.

Most small players resist systematization—seeing it as bureaucracy that stifles the creativity and speed that fueled their early success. They remain trapped in a perpetual startup phase, working harder rather than smarter as complexity increases. While they exhaust themselves fighting the same battles repeatedly, system builders—the Napoleons of scalability—create self-reinforcing structures that multiply their impact beyond their direct reach.

In the digital economy, this principle becomes even more critical. A software startup with brilliant code but poor deployment systems can't scale. An e-commerce brand with compelling products but inconsistent customer experience can't grow. The modern equivalent of Napoleon's administrative reforms might be automated workflows, documented APIs, or scalable cloud architecture—different tools, same strategic imperative.

The edge isn't working harder—it's building smarter. Replacing heroic efforts with systematic approaches. Transforming personal knowledge into organizational capability. Creating structures that harness human nature rather than fighting it.

Systems aren't about rigidity—they're about reliable flexibility. They don't replace judgment; they embed it in processes that can scale beyond the limits of individual capacity.

THE MACHINERY OF GROWTH

Miami, November 2026. Alex Harper stands before a whiteboard covered in flowcharts. Around the conference table sit his expanded team: Emily handling operations, Javier overseeing production, plus five new faces—department heads for sourcing, marketing, delivery, finance, and design.

"This is holding us back," Alex says, pointing to a diagram showing their current production process. "Everything still runs through me or Javier. It worked at fifty thousand a month. It's breaking at five hundred thousand."

The company has grown explosively since their Sunrise Café success. Thirty employees now. A 15,000-square-foot production facility. Clients across Florida. But with growth has come growing pains—missed deadlines, quality inconsistencies, communication breakdowns.

"We're still operating like a garage workshop," Alex continues. "We need systems that scale."

Over the next month, they rebuild the company's operational backbone. Alex studies process engineering, reads case studies of manufacturing firms, consults with a business systems expert. The lessons of Napoleon's administrative reforms echo in his approach.

First, they document every process—from sourcing to delivery—that was previously locked in Alex and Javier's heads. Knowledge trapped in minds becomes knowledge embedded in systems.

"If you get hit by a bus tomorrow," Alex tells Javier, "the company should still know how to build our products."

Javier grumbles but complies, spending weeks documenting joinery techniques, finish applications, quality standards. They create a digital knowledge base using Notion, with video demonstrations for complex techniques and searchable documentation for materials and measurements.

They redesign the sourcing system, moving from reactive purchasing to strategic supply chain management. Teresa, the new sourcing director, establishes relationships with reclaimed wood suppliers across the Americas—creating redundancy where previously a single source failure could cripple production.

"No single point of failure," Alex emphasizes. "Napoleon's army had multiple supply routes. So should we."

For production, they implement a modified Toyota Production System approach—visualizing workflow, establishing quality checkpoints, creating feedback loops to identify and resolve bottlenecks. Craftspeople who formerly handled entire pieces now specialize in specific stages, improving consistency and speed. They integrate project management software that tracks each piece from order to delivery, with automated notifications when tasks lag behind schedule.

The most controversial change: standardized design parameters. Javier resists fiercely.

"This kills creativity," he argues during a tense meeting. "We're not making IKEA crap."

"It's not about limiting design," Alex counters. "It's about creating a framework that makes execution reliable. Form follows function—and function needs structure."

The debate continues for days before they reach compromise: core structural elements standardize for consistency while aesthetic elements remain flexible for creativity. Just as Napoleon standardized administration but allowed local implementation, they create a system that balances reliability with adaptability.

Throughout the transformation, Alex balances centralization with autonomy—another Napoleonic lesson. Core standards apply company-wide, but department heads receive authority to implement within their domains.

"Clear objectives, flexible methods," becomes their mantra.

Emily creates a financial dashboard that provides real-time visibility into cash flow, inventory costs, and profit margins by product line. For the first time, they can see exactly where money flows through the business.

"What gets measured gets managed," Alex says, quoting Peter Drucker. "This dashboard gives us the metrics we need to make strategic decisions instead of just reacting."

By January 2027, the new systems are operational. Production capacity doubles while defect rates fall. Delivery timelines become reliable. Employee onboarding accelerates as documented processes replace ad-hoc training.

The ultimate test comes in March, when a Nicaraguan supplier's entire shipment of reclaimed teak—earmarked for a $150,000 corporate headquarters project—arrives water-damaged and unusable.

Pre-systems, this would have created crisis. Now, their supply chain redundancy kicks in. Teresa activates backup suppliers in Colombia and Brazil. Production adjusts scheduling through their visualization board. The client receives proactive communication and updated timeline.

"The wood is still bad," Alex tells the team. "But our response isn't."

They deliver the project two weeks late but to specification. The client—impressed by their transparent handling of the situation—signs a $180,000 follow-on contract.

The real validation comes a week later, when Alex takes his first vacation in three years. For seven days, he's completely disconnected—no calls, no emails, no emergency texts.

He returns to find operations running smoothly, decisions made appropriately, and progress continuing in his absence.

"That," he tells Emily, "is what systems do. They extend your reach beyond your grasp."

By mid-2027, their systemization pays its greatest dividend: scalability. They open a second production facility in Tampa without Alex or Javier needing to be physically present. The documented processes, training programs, and quality controls transfer cleanly to the new location.

"We're not just building furniture anymore," Alex tells his leadership team. "We're building a machine that builds furniture. Like how Netflix isn't just creating shows, but a system that reliably produces quality content."

Javier, initially the most resistant to systematization, gradually becomes its strongest advocate as he sees how structure enhances rather than limits craftsmanship.

"I used to spend all day fixing problems," he admits. "Now I can focus on what I do best."

In a quiet moment, reviewing monthly performance metrics that now run like clockwork, Alex reflects on the transformation.

THE SYSTEMS DIAGNOSTIC

Is your operation ready for systematic growth? Answer these critical questions to identify your most urgent needs:

Knowledge Dependency
Can work continue if key people are absent?
Is crucial information documented or just "in someone's head"?
Would a new team member know what to do without extensive training?

Quality Consistency
Do similar tasks produce similar outcomes regardless of who performs them?
Can you predict the quality of your output with confidence?
Are errors typically random or recurring patterns?

Scaling Capacity
Does increasing volume break your current processes?
Do you spend more time fighting fires than improving operations?
Can you double production without doubling your stress?

Decision Velocity
How many decisions require your personal attention?

Are routine choices made quickly and consistently throughout the organization?

Do you have clear criteria for when to escalate decisions versus handle locally?

Adaptation Capability

Can your operation respond to disruptions without crisis?

Do you have redundancies for critical functions?

How quickly can you implement changes across the organization?

Score yourself from 1 (weak) to 5 (strong) in each dimension. Areas scoring below 3 represent your most urgent systems needs.

Like Alex's furniture business before systematization, many operations function through heroic individual efforts until crisis forces change. The strongest organizations build systems before they're desperately needed—turning potential breaking points into breakthrough moments.

THE SYSTEMS CONNECTION

The empire builder and the entrepreneur reached the same crucial realization: enduring impact comes not from personal brilliance alone, but from embedding that brilliance in systems that function independently. Both recognized that the transition from conquering to governing requires fundamentally different approaches.

Napoleon's conquest of Europe demonstrated his tactical genius, but his administrative reformation of France revealed his strategic vision. The Napoleonic Code didn't just unify legal contradictions; it created a framework that balanced clarity with adaptability. His administrative reforms didn't just improve efficiency; they built self-reinforcing structures that channeled self-interest toward collective goals. By designing systems that worked with human nature rather than against it, he created frameworks that survived his fall.

Alex's business growth showed his entrepreneurial talent, but his systematization of operations demonstrated his leadership maturity.

The production processes didn't just document existing knowledge; they transformed personal expertise into organizational capability. The supply chain redundancies didn't just prevent crises; they created resilience against unpredictable challenges. By building structures that balanced standardization with flexibility, he created a company that could function beyond his direct control.

Systems aren't about replacing judgment with automation—they're about embedding good judgment into frameworks that can scale. Napoleon didn't eliminate the need for talented administrators; he created structures that amplified their impact and aligned their incentives. Alex didn't remove craftsmanship from furniture production; he built processes that made quality more consistent and less dependent on heroic efforts.

Both understood that true leadership isn't measured by personal indispensability but by organizational capability that functions in your absence. Napoleon's administrative systems continued influencing Europe long after his exile. Alex's operational frameworks enabled his company to function smoothly during his first real vacation.

That's the edge you need—not making yourself irreplaceable, but building structures that extend your vision beyond your reach. Understanding that the ultimate measure of leadership isn't what happens when you're present, but what happens when you're not.

THE TAKEAWAY

Build the machine, not just the product. Systems outlast their creators and multiply their impact.

Napoleon's Code survived his defeat at Waterloo. Alex's processes weathered a major supply crisis. You scale through structure, not just effort.

Your advantage isn't working harder—it's building smarter. The market eventually outgrows individual heroics, no matter how brilliant. When complexity increases beyond personal capacity, systems become the only sustainable path forward.

Document the implicit knowledge in your head. Create redundancies where single points of failure exist. Implement feedback mechanisms that surface problems before they become crises. Balance standardization for consistency with flexibility for adaptation.

Systems aren't about bureaucracy—they're about leverage. They don't constrain creativity; they channel it productively. They don't replace human judgment; they amplify it across more decisions than any individual could make.

The most important question isn't "Can I solve this problem?" but "Can I create a system that solves this category of problems repeatedly without my intervention?"

Personal brilliance conquers. Systematic brilliance endures.

Chapter 10: The Human Factor - Allies or Knives

"Friendship is but a name; I love no one, not even my brothers."
—Napoleon Bonaparte, Letter to Josephine, 1796

THE ALLIANCE LABYRINTH

Tilsit, June 1807. A raft floats in the middle of the Niemen River. Two emperors meet where neither controls the territory—neutral water between armies.

Napoleon Bonaparte clasps hands with Tsar Alexander I of Russia. Yesterday's enemy becomes today's ally with the stroke of a pen. A peace treaty divides Europe between them. French troops will leave Russian borders. Russian ships will join the Continental System against Britain.

"I hate the English as much as you do," Alexander tells Napoleon.

Napoleon smiles, unconvinced. But the alliance serves both their interests—for now.

This is Napoleon's pattern—relationships as strategic instruments, alliances as temporary conveniences. From his earliest campaigns, he recognized that empire-building requires more than military might. It demands a complex web of connections, carefully managed.

Some serve him well. Marshal Ney, "the bravest of the brave," follows him with doglike loyalty through triumph and disaster. Marshal Murat, his flamboyant cavalry commander and brother-in-law, secures his flanks in a hundred battles.

Others become liabilities. His brother Joseph, installed as King of Spain, proves incompetent against Spanish resistance. Marshal Bernadotte, adopted into the Swedish royal family, eventually turns against him and joins the coalition that brings him down.

"Put my brothers on thrones and they forget whose power put them there," Napoleon complains to his secretary during the Spanish debacle of 1808.

Spain reveals the limits of imposed alliance. Where French armies march, Spanish guerrillas emerge from the population—invisible enemies cutting supply lines, ambushing patrols, bleeding the occupation through a thousand cuts.

"In open battle, I can defeat any army," Napoleon admits. "But how does one defeat a people who refuse to acknowledge defeat?"

Even his closest relationships bend to strategic necessity. When his beloved Josephine fails to produce an heir, he divorces her to marry Marie-Louise of Austria—a political alliance that delivers him a son but costs him his most devoted supporter.

Only a handful of advisors earn his genuine trust. Louis-Alexandre Berthier, his chief of staff, translates Napoleon's rapid-fire commands into clear orders. Jean-Baptiste Bernadotte, his police minister, builds the intelligence network that secures his rule at home.

Yet even as he uses relationships instrumentally, Napoleon understands their genuine power. Josephine's charm softens diplomatic negotiations with Prussia. Marie-Louise's Habsburg connections temporarily neutralize Austrian hostility. Marshal Ney's personal courage inspires loyalty throughout the army.

At Tilsit, watching Alexander carefully, Napoleon recognizes the same calculation behind the Tsar's warm words. This alliance, like all his alliances, will last only as long as mutual interest sustains it.

Four years later, he invades Russia. Alexander, once his "brother" in peace, becomes his most determined enemy. Their Tilsit alliance shatters into the bloodiest campaign of Napoleon's career—proving that relationships built solely on temporary advantage collapse when those advantages shift.

In exile on St. Helena, reviewing his fallen empire, Napoleon reflects on the human factor that statistics and strategies often overlook.

"In the end," he tells his last companions, "it was not armies but alliances that determined my fate. When I managed them well, Europe trembled. When I managed them poorly, I fell."

Surveying the ruins of his empire from exile, he reflects coldly:

"Men are loyal to their interests above all else. I understood this—I simply failed to make their interests permanently align with mine."

THE RELATIONSHIP CALCULUS

Every empire rests on a foundation of relationships.

Behind the vision, beyond the strategy, beneath the systems lies the human factor that ultimately determines whether you rise or fall. The connections you forge, maintain, or sever create the network through which opportunity flows or danger enters.

Relationships function simultaneously as amplifiers and constraints. The right allies multiply your impact beyond your direct reach; the wrong ones drain resources while delivering little value. Strategic partners open doors that would remain closed to individual effort; betrayals from within can collapse structures no external force could topple.

Napoleon's conquests demonstrated his military genius, but his alliance strategy revealed both his diplomatic brilliance and his relational blind spots. His transactional approach to human connections—valuing people primarily for their utility—built his empire rapidly but undermined its stability. When interests shifted, so did loyalties, leaving him vulnerable precisely when he needed support most.

That's the essence of the relationship calculus: recognizing that while all professional relationships contain transactional elements, the strongest alliances blend mutual interest with genuine investment beyond immediate return. They balance strategic value with human connection, calculation with trust.

Most small players make one of two critical errors in relationships. Either they operate with naive trust, forming partnerships based on personality without strategic alignment, or they function with such ruthless calculation that they generate value but not loyalty. They fail to recognize that the most powerful relationships serve both strategic and human dimensions.

In the digital economy, this principle becomes even more essential. A SaaS founder might secure API partnerships with major platforms, but if those relationships remain purely transactional, a change in terms of service can destroy the business overnight. A content creator might build a massive following on a single platform, only to discover how fragile that one-dimensional relationship becomes when algorithms change.

The edge isn't manipulation or blind faith—it's strategic authenticity. The ability to form connections grounded in genuine mutual benefit while recognizing that all alliances have limits. To invest in relationships beyond their immediate return without forgetting that interests ultimately drive actions.

In the complex terrain of human connections, neither cynicism nor idealism provides reliable maps. The path forward requires both clear-eyed assessment of interests and genuine investment in shared success.

THE NETWORK NEXUS

Miami, September 2027. Alex Harper's office overlooks their expanded production facility. Through glass walls, he watches thirty craftspeople transform reclaimed wood into furniture for clients across Florida. The company now generates $450,000 monthly revenue with consistent profitability.

But today, that growth trajectory faces its greatest threat.

"Gables Hardware is backing out," Emily says, sliding a letter across his desk. "Effective immediately."

Alex reads the notice with growing disbelief. Gables Hardware—their retail partner for two years—is terminating their relationship without warning. Six display locations, gone. Twenty percent of monthly revenue, vanished overnight.

"What happened?"

Emily's expression tightens. "They've partnered with Stellar Office Supplies—Monarch's furniture division."

The same competitor from years ago, now fully absorbed into Monarch Development's expanding empire. Jorge Mendez has finally found a way to cut them off from a key distribution channel.

Later that day, Alex gathers his leadership team: Emily, Javier, and the five department heads who now manage daily operations. The mood is grim as he outlines the situation.

"We've relied too heavily on one retail partner," he admits. "That stops now."

Over the next week, they assess their relationship portfolio—mapping every client, supplier, partner, and competitor in their network. The analysis reveals uncomfortable truths. Their business has grown, but their relationship strategy hasn't evolved with it.

"We're still operating like the underdog," Alex realizes. "Reacting to opportunities rather than cultivating strategic relationships."

Napoleon's alliance strategy offers insights, but also warnings. The Emperor's purely transactional approach to relationships ultimately left him vulnerable when circumstances changed. Alex wants something more sustainable.

"We need partners, not just channels," he tells the team. "Relationships where both sides have skin in the game."

They identify two critical relationship targets: a partner with retail reach to replace Gables Hardware, and a strategic alliance that can open new markets beyond Miami.

For retail, Alex approaches the South Florida Garden Club Association—a network of twelve garden centers across three counties. Rather than a standard vendor arrangement, he proposes a genuine partnership: custom-designed outdoor furniture made from weather-resistant reclaimed wood, with both companies' branding and a revenue-sharing model.

"Instead of paying for shelf space, we become part of their identity," Alex explains to the association's board. "Your customers already care about sustainability. Our products tell that story through your brand."

In parallel, he explores a digital partnership with GardenWorld, an up-and-coming content creator with 500,000 followers passionate about sustainable outdoor living. Like partnering with a rising star whose audience perfectly aligns with their values, the relationship brings both opportunity and unpredictability.

The negotiations with both partners take three intense weeks. Unlike previous deals where Alex focused purely on terms, he invests in understanding the garden centers' broader challenges—seasonal revenue fluctuations, competition from big-box stores, changing customer demographics.

"Napoleon would have seen what they could do for him," Alex tells Emily after a particularly difficult session. "We need to see what we can solve for them."

The breakthrough comes when Alex invites the association's leadership to tour their production facility. Not a staged visit, but an honest look at their operation—including challenges and limitations.

"This is who we really are," he tells them, showing both their sophisticated systems and areas still being improved. "We're betting on transparency over perfection."

The vulnerability pays off. The garden centers sign a three-year partnership that not only replaces the lost Gables revenue but expands their outdoor furniture line into a new market segment.

For their strategic alliance, they target GreenWorks Architecture—a rising firm specializing in sustainable commercial spaces. Rather than a traditional vendor-client relationship, Alex proposes embedding one of their designers within the architecture firm to collaborate on projects from conception.

"We're not just selling you furniture," he tells GreenWorks' founders. "We're integrating our expertise into your design process."

This negotiation tests relationships within Alex's own team. Javier resists sending their lead designer to work inside another company.

"We're giving away our intellectual property," he argues.

"We're building a blood pact that can't be easily replaced," Alex counters. "Something Monarch can't just outbid."

The tension persists until they structure an arrangement that protects both companies' interests while creating mutual dependency—shared credit, split revenue on innovations, and a two-year exclusivity period.

One afternoon, Alex drives to Gables Hardware, determined to confront its owner directly about the sudden termination. The conversation is uncomfortable, raw.

"Two years of partnership, cut off without warning," he says, keeping his voice steady despite his anger.

The owner, a man in his sixties who built the chain from nothing, doesn't meet his eyes. "Monarch offered exclusivity payments we couldn't refuse," he admits. "This business is my retirement."

Alex feels both understanding and disappointment. "You built something real," he says. "Now you're selling its soul."

"Maybe," the owner responds. "But my grandkids will go to college. Would you choose differently?"

Alex leaves without an answer. Some relationships can't be saved once interests diverge too far.

As his new relationships develop, Alex also reinvests in his core team. The company has grown beyond the days when he, Emily, and Javier handled everything, but their foundation remains critical.

"Napoleon treated his marshals as instruments," Alex tells Emily during a rare quiet moment. "That's why some betrayed him when fortunes changed."

He creates an equity structure that gives long-term team members ownership stakes. Implements a profit-sharing system that aligns everyone's interests with company success. Establishes quarterly retreats where strategy discussions blend with genuine connection.

In November, their patience pays off. GreenWorks wins the contract to design Harbor Square—a waterfront development featuring restaurants, offices, and retail space. The project requirements include sustainable furnishings throughout the complex.

"This is a $287,500 opportunity," the GreenWorks principal tells Alex. "But only if you can handle the scale."

Because of their embedded designer, they've already developed concepts aligned with the architectural vision. Because of their garden center partnership, they have distribution channels for the retail spaces. Because of their systems, they can scale production without sacrificing quality.

"We've been building toward this for three years," Alex tells the team. "Not just the capacity—the relationships."

When they sign the contract, it represents more than revenue. It validates their evolved approach to the human factor—relationships built on strategic alignment and genuine investment rather than mere transaction.

In a moment of reflection, Alex thinks about the journey from his garage to this watershed moment. Each step required not just vision, strategy, or systems, but people willing to commit their talents to a shared goal.

"Napoleon conquered through force and fell when alliances shifted," he tells his leadership team during their contract celebration. "We're building something that grows stronger with each genuine connection."

Emily raises her glass. "To relationships that lift rather than cut."

THE RELATIONSHIP PORTFOLIO ASSESSMENT

Strategic relationships don't happen by accident. Evaluate your current connections using these five dimensions:

Strategic Alignment
Do your partners share complementary goals?
Are your values compatible in ways that matter?

Does success for them mean success for you?

Dependency Risk

What percentage of revenue flows through a single relationship?

Could any partner's decision cripple your operation?

Do alternatives exist if key relationships fail?

Value Exchange

Is the relationship balanced or one-sided?

Are both parties receiving meaningful benefits?

Does the relationship create value beyond the transactional?

Investment Depth

Have you invested in the relationship beyond immediate return?

Do interactions extend beyond strictly necessary business matters?

Would the relationship survive a short-term misalignment of interests?

Growth Potential

Can this relationship evolve as you both grow?

Are there unexplored opportunities for collaboration?

Does the relationship open doors to new connections?

For each key relationship, score these dimensions from 1 (weak) to 5 (strong). Relationships scoring below 3 in multiple areas represent your greatest vulnerabilities—or your most significant opportunities for reinforcement.

Like Alex's relationship with Gables Hardware, many partnerships that seem stable can collapse when tested. The strongest connections combine mutual value with genuine investment that makes separation costly to both sides.

THE HUMAN CONNECTION

The empire builder and the entrepreneur both discovered that relationships ultimately determine destiny. Their different approaches to human connection yield different results—one a meteoric rise and fall, the other a more sustainable growth.

Napoleon's alliance strategy demonstrated both brilliance and fatal flaws. At Tilsit, he negotiated a peace with Russia that temporarily secured his eastern flank, allowing him to focus elsewhere. But his fundamentally transactional view of relationships—valuing people primarily for their utility—undermined long-term stability. When he placed his brothers on foreign thrones based on blood rather than competence, their failures in Spain and elsewhere created vulnerabilities. When he divorced Josephine for political advantage, he lost not just a wife but a skilled diplomatic partner whose charm had smoothed many negotiations.

Alex's relationship evolution showed both strategic calculation and growing emotional intelligence. The garden center partnership created retail presence that Monarch couldn't easily disrupt, addressing the vulnerability revealed by Gables Hardware's defection. But unlike Napoleon, Alex recognized that sustainable relationships require investment beyond immediate return. By exposing real operational challenges to potential partners, embedding team members in allied organizations, and creating mutual dependencies that served both parties' interests, he built connections more resistant to competitive pressure or changing circumstances.

The contrast isn't about naivety versus cynicism. Both men recognized that interests drive actions and that all professional relationships contain transactional elements. The difference lies in whether transaction defines the relationship's limits or merely establishes its beginning.

Napoleon's greatest vulnerability emerged from relationships that remained purely strategic—when circumstances changed, so did loyalties. Alex's greatest strength developed from relationships that began with strategic alignment but grew beyond immediate utility— creating resilience against changing market conditions.

That's the edge you need—not just forming connections based on current value, but investing in relationships that can evolve as circumstances change. Understanding that while interests matter, trust built through genuine investment creates bonds that pure calculation cannot match.

THE TAKEAWAY

Forge deep alliances, not mere transactions. Strategic relationships determine your ceiling and your floor.

Napoleon manipulated alliances but fell when they shifted. Alex cultivated partnerships that strengthened with time. You grow through connections that blend strategic value with genuine investment.

Your advantage isn't exploitation but alignment—finding partners whose success directly feeds yours and vice versa. The market rewards those who build relationships resistant to competitive disruption and changing circumstances.

Assess your relationship portfolio regularly. Identify vulnerable single points of failure. Develop connections with both strategic utility and authentic investment. Create mutual dependencies that serve all parties' interests.

Purely transactional relationships are easily replaced when better terms appear elsewhere. The most valuable connections blend mutual benefit with shared identity—partnerships where separation would cost both sides more than just revenue.

Napoleon's empire expanded through forced alliances but collapsed when those alliances broke under pressure. Alex's company grew through partnerships where both sides remained committed even when competitors offered alternatives.

When you find partners who multiply your impact, invest beyond the immediate return. The relationships that truly transform your trajectory are those that evolve from transaction to trust—connections where both sides choose to remain loyal not just because it's profitable, but because it's personal.

Empires rise through vision and strategy, but they endure through relationships that weather both crisis and success.

Conclusion: Napoleon's Edge, Your Enterprise

From $200 to $2.5 million. That's the journey—from Alex Harper's wobbly desk to a sustainable enterprise that transforms how people think about furniture, work, and environmental responsibility. The same strategic principles that carried Napoleon from artillery captain to emperor drove this modern conquest.

This journey—from vision to sustainable venture—follows a path blazed by history's greatest strategists but tailored for today's builder. Different fields, different scales, same principles. Napoleon's edge, translated for your market.

THE CONQUEST FRAMEWORK

Vision. Strategy. Speed. These three forces drive breakthrough opportunities while others remain stuck in planning or paralysis.

Spot the Damn Gap - Napoleon saw what others missed at Toulon—a tactical opportunity others dismissed. Alex identified a niche that larger competitors overlooked. Both succeeded not through revolutionary ideas but by recognizing specific openings that matched their capabilities. Your edge: See the crack in existing markets and commit fully to exploiting it before others notice.

Outsmart, Don't Outspend - Napoleon outmaneuvered larger forces at Austerlitz through positioning and preparation. Alex competed with better-funded rivals by targeting specific pain points their advantages couldn't address. Your edge: Find the battlefield where your strengths matter more than your competitor's size.

Hit Before They Blink - Napoleon's lightning campaigns caught enemies unprepared. Alex rushed imperfect products to market, capturing opportunities before competitors mobilized. Your edge:

Launch now, fix later. The window of opportunity closes faster than perfection arrives.

THE LEADERSHIP IMPERATIVE

Vision without execution is hallucination. The second phase transforms individual hustle into organizational capability—the ability to inspire others to commit their talents to a shared goal.

Hold the Line, Heart and All - Napoleon inspired loyalty through shared hardship and delivered victories. Alex rallied his team through backyard demos and genuine commitment to their success. Your edge: Lead from the front, deliver victories that benefit all, and create purpose beyond personal gain.

Get Up, Swing Again - Napoleon returned from exile to reclaim power, transforming defeat into opportunity. Alex pivoted after Marco's betrayal, creating the Modulo line that opened new markets. Your edge: Treat failure as a detour, not a destination. Respond to setbacks with strategic adaptation, not just persistence.

Master Ambition's Edge - Napoleon's overreach in Russia demonstrated how unchecked ambition becomes self-destructive. Alex's premature leap to a luxury showroom nearly collapsed his company before he course-corrected. Your edge: Push boundaries but recognize limits. Ambition requires governance to remain productive.

THE EMPIRE ARCHITECTURE

The final phase builds sustainable structures—value that extends beyond personal capacity and endures beyond immediate circumstances.

Spin It, Own It - Napoleon controlled his narrative through strategic communication. Alex created authentic content that reframed imperfections as evidence of sustainability. Your edge: Control your narrative or others will define it for you. Shape perception through strategic emphasis of truth.

Buy the Win - Napoleon secured his coup by understanding what truly motivated each key player. Alex won critical partnerships by recognizing deeper values beyond money. Your edge: Identify what truly drives decisions, not just what people claim motivates them. Create alignment where everyone's interests are genuinely served.

Build the Machine - Napoleon created administrative frameworks that outlasted his rule. Alex systematized operations to function without his constant intervention. Your edge: Create processes that capture your expertise but don't require your presence. Systems transform personal capability into organizational capacity.

Lock in Strategic Allies - Napoleon's transactional approach to alliances ultimately left him vulnerable. Alex built partnerships based on mutual dependency and genuine investment. Your edge: Form connections that blend strategic value with authentic investment. Transform transactions into meaningful bonds.

THE MODERN MASTER

Elon Musk embodies these principles across multiple industries. He spotted gaps others dismissed in online payments (PayPal), electric vehicles (Tesla), and space launch (SpaceX). His strategic positioning made "sustainability" and "innovation" inseparable in consumers' minds. When faced with near-bankruptcy at both Tesla and SpaceX, he pivoted with ruthless resilience. His systems thinking created scalable approaches to manufacturing and innovation.

Musk isn't perfect—his ambition sometimes outpaces execution, particularly with bold timeline promises. But his application of these strategic principles in digital, manufacturing, and infrastructure ventures proves their versatility across domains.

The principles work whether you're building software or physical products, running a solo consultancy or scaling a team, launching a side hustle or transforming an industry. Digital tools amplify their impact: cloud-based SOPs replace the Napoleonic Code; analytics dashboards serve as modern intelligence networks; automated workflows become your administrative framework.

YOUR BATTLEFIELD

Start where you are. Napoleon began as an outsider with a thick accent and few connections. Alex started with $500 and a garage. Your current limitations aren't barriers—they're the specific conditions that will shape your unique approach.

If you're just beginning:

What specific gap exists that others dismiss but aligns with your capabilities?
Where can you compete on positioning rather than resources?
What imperfect offering could you launch this week instead of perfecting endlessly?

If you're leading a team:

How are you demonstrating commitment through presence and shared struggle?
When setbacks occur, how quickly do you pivot versus perseverate?
What guardrails have you established to keep ambition productive?

If you're building for longevity:

What narrative are you actively controlling versus surrendering to others?
How deeply do you understand what truly motivates your key stakeholders?
Which systems have you created that extend your impact beyond your direct control?

NEXT ACTIONS

Map Your Gap - Identify one specific opportunity others are missing that matches your unique capabilities. Commit to exploiting it within the next 14 days.

Document One Process - Choose your most frequently repeated task. Document it so thoroughly that someone else could perform it without your involvement.

Strengthen One Alliance - Select your most strategically valuable relationship. Invest in it beyond immediate transaction by identifying and addressing their deeper motivations.

The edge comes not from knowing these principles but from applying them when others don't. From recognizing patterns across centuries and contexts. From understanding that success follows consistent dynamics regardless of field.

Napoleon ruled nations. Alex built a $2.5M sustainable enterprise. You're next—sharpen your edge.

NAPOLEON'S EDGE: BATTLEFIELD CHEAT SHEET

CONQUEST FRAMEWORK

The principles that drive opportunity identification and capture

"Spot the gap, take it first." (Vision)

"Impossible is a word found only in the dictionary of fools." — Napoleon

Action: Find one overlooked opportunity that aligns with your capabilities. Move on it this week.

"Outsmart, don't outspend." (Strategy)

"In war, three-quarters turns on personal character and one-quarter on the terrain." —Napoleon

Action: Identify where your competitor's size becomes a liability rather than strength.

"Strike fast, fix fast." (Speed)

"Take time to deliberate, but when the time for action arrives, stop thinking and go in." —Napoleon

Action: Launch an imperfect version today rather than a perfect version someday.

LEADERSHIP IMPERATIVE

The principles that transform individual effort into collective force

"Lead from the front." (Leadership)

"The leader is the arbiter of the people's fate." —Napoleon

Action: Share the hardest tasks with your team. Demonstrate what you ask others to do.

"Pivot from defeat." (Resilience)

"From triumph to downfall is but a step." —Napoleon

Action: When setbacks occur, assess what remains and rebuild within 48 hours.

"Aim high, not blind." (Ambition)

"Great ambition is the passion of a great character." —Napoleon

Action: Set specific guardrails that prevent your ambition from becoming self-destructive.

EMPIRE ARCHITECTURE

The principles that create sustainable structures beyond personal capacity

"Frame truth powerfully." (Perception)

"Four hostile newspapers are more to be feared than a thousand bayonets." —Napoleon

Action: Identify one narrative about your venture that others control and reclaim it.

"Identify true motivations." (Influence)

"A man will fight harder for his interests than for his rights." —Napoleon

Action: Determine what truly drives your three most important stakeholders beyond what they claim.

"Build the machine." (Systems)

"My maxim has always been: a career open to all talents, without distinction of birth." —Napoleon

Action: Document one process that currently depends entirely on you but shouldn't.

"Forge deep alliances, not mere transactions." (Relationships)

"In the end, it was not armies but alliances that determined my fate." —Napoleon

Action: Identify one transactional relationship that could deliver more value if given authentic investment.

DAILY COMMAND

Which battlefield principle does your current situation demand most?

What specific action will you take today to apply it?

How will you measure whether that application succeeded?

"Napoleon ruled nations. Alex built sustainable enterprise. You can too—sharpen your edge."

www.ingramcontent.com/pod-product-compliance
Lightning Source LLC
Chambersburg PA
CBHW050113060525
26241CB00016B/58